Arithmetricks

Second Edition

More Than 100 AMAZING Math Tricks

Jeri S. Cipriano

Good Year Books

Tucson, Arizona

Dedication

For the number one family in my life: Bill, Rachel, Marco, and Max, and in loving memory of my mother, on whom we've always counted.

A Note to Parents and Teachers

This book encourages a child's enthusiasm for hands-on fun while building important math skills in subtle ways. The creative activities are unlike textbook drills, yet they, too, provide practice with computations, following directions, logic, problem-solving, visual discrimination, graphs, patterns, proportions, shapes, time, and measurements.

Children who are motivated to engage, to take risks, to "stretch," will, no doubt, have their efforts rewarded by a deeper understanding of and appreciation for math. They'll probably find an improvement in school math as well, which comes as the result of increased confidence, interest, and practice.

Whenever possible, encourage math activities at home, such as reading sports scores and stats, following recipes, building and doing crafts, making graphs and charts, working on puzzles, and so on. Whenever kids experience the thrill of cracking a code or making a discovery, they will be reinforcing their love of math mystery.

Good Year Books

Our titles are available for most basic curriculum subjects plus many enrichment areas. For information on other Good Year Books and to place orders, contact your local bookseller or educational dealer, or visit our website at www.goodyearbooks.com. For a complete catalog, please contact:

Good Year Books
PO Box 91858
Tucson, AZ 85752-1858
www.goodyearbooks.com

Cover Design: Dan Miedaner
Cover Illustrations: Corasue Nicholas (back cover, "dressed to the nines") and Nancy Rudd
Text Design: Meyers Design, Inc.
2nd edition revision by Doug Goewey
Illustrations: Nancy Rudd
Additional Illustrations: Corasue Nicholas (pages 15, 18, 32, 38, 62, 87, 102, 105 [dog])

Contents

For Openers: Math Counts! 1

Arithmetricks: Number Stunts 3

Mental Math: Mind Benders and More 33

Math Works: Music, Language, Art, History 39

Math Matters: Fun Fare 63

In Good Shape: Geometry and Patterns 81

Hands-on Math: Things to Make and Do 93

Time and Money: Tidbits, Rib Ticklers, and Coin Tricks 103

Calculator Math: Enter Laughing 117

Let the Games Begin: Paper, Pencils, and Partners 129

The Finish Line: Celebrate with a Mathathon! 143

Answer Key 154

Preface

Be a mind reader . . . decode secret messages . . . learn magic!

With just this book, a pencil, and some paper, you can spend googols of fun time! *Googols!!?* Did someone say *googols?* Yes, using just that one word will impress people. (See page 29.) Do you want to really amaze your friends? Would you like to stump a few teachers, too? Then check out the tricks, puzzles, and facts in this book.

You can see that this book is nothing like a textbook. But all the activities have to do with math. You can start anywhere or skip around. You'll probably find that the more fun you have with this book, the better you'll do in math. So sharpen your pencils and get set to find the answers to these questions and more!

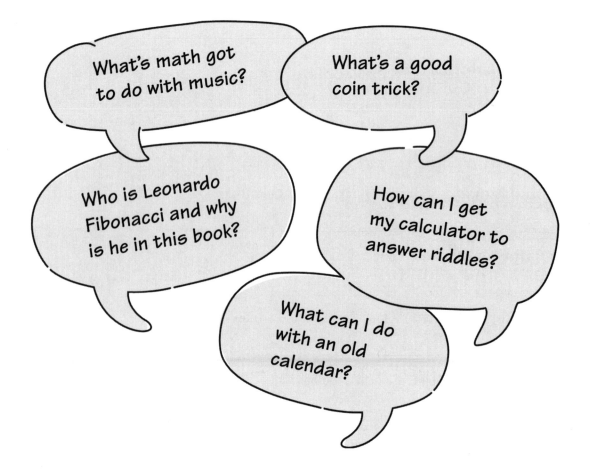

For Openers: Math Counts!

Each year you study math in school. Did you ever wonder why? Questions about math may not be up front in your head. Still, you'll probably find these facts interesting.

How old is math?

Math is the study of numbers, shapes, and space. Did they do math in ancient times? You bet! In fact, math goes w-a-y back—all the way back to the beginning of the human race. You may wonder why cave people needed math 10,000 years ago. But remember: Even cave people had to keep track of their food and belongings.

What was early math like?

No one knows for sure who first used math. But people throughout time have needed math to help solve problems. The first math was some kind of counting system. Then, when people started farming, they needed calendars to mark time and note the seasons for planting.

How did math keep up with people?

People began making things by hand. They began building. They needed tools. They needed weapons to protect themselves. Counting was not enough. Now people needed to know how to measure and calculate. Pretty soon, people started adding, subtracting, multiplying, and dividing. Then fractions were added.

How did math continue to grow?

Around 300 B.C., a man named Euclid wrote a series of books in ancient Greece that laid the foundation for much of the *geometry* that we still use today. Geometry is the study of shapes and angles. People needed geometry to learn about sizes and shapes. They needed geometry to measure land and to build great monuments.

As business and industry grew, money was invented, and, later, clocks were created to measure the business day.

At sea, sailors first used the stars to help guide them across oceans. Later, *trigonometry* made their work more accurate. (Trigonometry is the study of distances and directions.) *Algebra*, the study of variables and the operations of arithmetic with variables, developed over time. Algebra—the way it is done today—began in 1591 when French mathematician François Viète used letters of the alphabet to describe patterns.

How are science and math related?

As the field of science grew, so did math. Understanding gravity or how the Moon orbits the Earth or the speed of a rocket ship requires calculations. Sir Isaac Newton invented *calculus* to help scientists deal with these complicated issues. Scientists also rely on math to study the human body in its smallest parts. Albert Einstein's mathematics helped unlock the secrets of the atom and advanced science's study of life.

Do we have all the math we need now?

Today, computers are helping us solve problems faster than ever before. But the human race keeps developing. Some day new questions will arise and people will look to math for the answers. New branches of math will grow out of our need to find solutions to the challenges that lie ahead. One thing is sure. When it comes to advancing the human race, math *counts!*

Arithmetricks:
Number Stunts

In this section, you'll find enough number tricks for several magic shows. You'll leave your audience speechless when you provide instant answers, read their minds, and perform extraordinary number feats. You'll also learn how to create magic squares and fun figures and do interesting tricks with calendars. Are you ready for a good time? Then, go figure!

Time to Show Off

You'll stun your audience with these magic number tricks.

Just "Four" You

Give a friend the following directions:

- Write a three-digit number.

- Mix up the digits to get another three-digit number.

- Subtract the smaller numbers from the larger.

- Add the digits in the difference. (If you get a two-digit answer, add the two digits to get a single digit.)

- Subtract 5 to get a final number.

Now put your hand to your forehead and look like you're concentrating. Then say: "Your number is 4!" (Try it. It works every time.)

I've Got Your Number

Write the number 7 on a piece of paper and keep it in your pocket. Then give the following directions:

- Think of a number from 1 through 99.

- Double your number.

- Add 5.

- Add 12.

- Subtract 3.

- Divide it in half.

- Subtract your original number.

Take out the paper from your pocket. Say, "Your number is 7!" Show the paper to your friend to really impress him or her.

Suppose your friend picks the number 384.

384
483
483 − 384 = 99
9 + 9 = 18
1 + 8 = 9
9 − 5 = 4

Suppose your friend picks the number 54.

54
54 + 54 = 108
108 + 5 = 113
113 + 12 = 125
125 − 3 = 122
122 ÷ 2 = 61
61 − 54 = 7

One Up!

Try this one yourself. Then share it with a friend.

- Write a three-digit number in which the three digits are consecutive.

- Multiply the largest digit by the smallest.

- Now multiply the middle digit by itself.

What do you notice?

Suppose you pick the number 345.

345

3 x 5 = 15

4 x 4 = 16

Now try these numbers.
567 234 123 789

What do you notice?

Fun Fact

No matter how many times you multiply 1 by itself, you'll always get 1. That can't be said for any other number.

Gotcha!

Here are five more mind-reading tricks.

1. On a sheet of paper; write this "magic number": 12,345,679.

- Ask a friend for a number from 1 through 9. In your head, multiply your friend's number by 9. Write down the answer.

- Now have your friend multiply the magic number by the number you just wrote.

- SURPRISE! The answer will be made up entirely of the number your friend gave you.

2. Tell your friend the following:

- Choose a number from 1 through 5.
- Double it.
- Add 2.
- Divide by 2.
- Subtract your original number.

Say: "The answer is 1!"

1. Suppose your friend picks the number 2.

2

$2 \times 9 = 18$

$12,345,679 \times 18 = 222,222,222$

2. Suppose your friend picks the number 3.

3

$3 \times 2 = 6$

$6 + 2 = 8$

$8 \div 2 = 4$

$4 - 3 = 1$

3. *Tell your friend:*

- Think of a number—any number:
- Multiply your number by 2.
- Add 4.
- Divide by 2.
- Subtract your original number.

Say, "The answer is 2!"

4. *Tell your friend:*

- Write a number:
- Add 9.
- Multiply by 2.
- Subtract 4.
- Divide by 2.
- Subtract your original number.

Say: "The answer is 7!"

5. *Tell your friend:*

- Think of a number from 1 through 100.
- Multiply your number by 3.
- Add 6 to that number.
- Divide that number by 3.

Ask your friend what that number is. All you have to do is subtract 2 from that number to get your friend's original number.

3. Suppose your friend picks the number 65.

65
65 x 2 = 130
130 + 4 = 134
134 ÷ 2 = 67
67 – 65 = 2

4. Suppose your friend picks the number 109.

109
109 + 9 = 118
118 x 2 = 236
236 – 4 = 232
232 ÷ 2 = 116
116 – 109 = 7

5. Suppose your friend picks the number 50.

50
50 x 3 = 150
150 + 6 = 156
156 ÷ 3 = 52
52 – 2 = 50

Out of Their Minds Math!

Now this trick is guaranteed to drive your friends crazy. No matter what they do, the answer will always be 1,089!

First, write the number 1,089 on a piece of paper and put it in a friend's pocket. Then tell your friend that, no matter what he or she does, you'll be able to guess the final answer.

1. Tell your friend to write any three-digit number, but to make sure that the digit in the hundreds place is at least 2 greater than the digit in the ones place.

2. Now tell your friend to reverse the digits in the number.

3. Next, tell him or her to subtract the smaller number from the larger number.

4. Have your friend reverse the digits in the answer to #3. Add the resulting number to the answer for #3.

Now for the big moment: Tell your friend to look at the paper you've hidden. You can't go wrong. The result will be 1,089—every time!

Suppose your friend picks the number 431.

431

134

$431 - 134 = 297$

792

$792 + 297 = 1,089$

Hi, Five!

In this trick, it's impossible to say, "Bye, five!"

- Write any three-digit number.

- Add that number to the next consecutive number.

- Add 9 to the total.

- Divide your answer by 2.

- Subtract your original number from the answer.

Choose different three-digit numbers and repeat the process. Don't be surprised if you get 5 each time.

Suppose you pick the number 653.

653

653 + 654 = 1,307

1,307 + 9 = 1,316

1,316 ÷ 2 = 658

658 − 653 = 5

HIGH
FIVE

Hi, Five!

Take Five

The "Sixth" Sense Trick

Tell a friend to choose an odd number between 1 and 50 that is divisible by 5. When your friend tells the number, pretend to concentrate. Then pull out a note with the same number on it.

The Secret

Ahead of time, prepare five slips of paper. Write one of these numbers on each slip of paper: 5, 15, 25, 35, 45. These numbers are the *only* odd numbers between 1 and 50 that are divisible by 5.

Hide the slips of paper on you (up a sleeve, in a pocket, in a shoe, in a belt, and so on). Remember where each number is. Your friend will be amazed when you produce the correct answer, as if by magic!

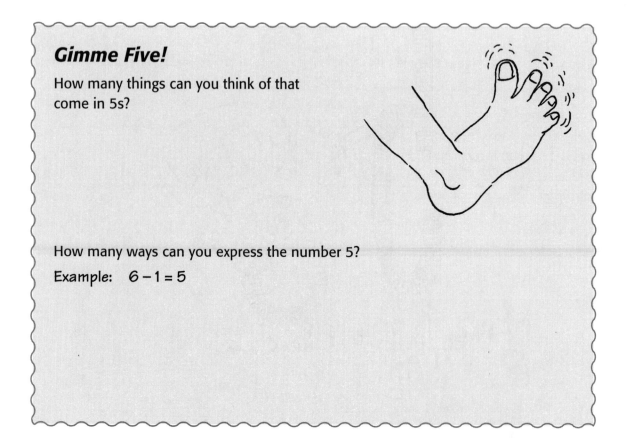

Gimme Five!

How many things can you think of that come in 5s?

How many ways can you express the number 5?

Example: 6 − 1 = 5

Seven Up!

No matter what you do, you will always come up with seven. Don't believe it? Try it as many times as you like.

Directions:

- Choose any number and write it.

- Double that number.

- Add 5.

- Add 12 more.

- Now subtract 3.

- Finally, divide by 2.

- Now subtract your original number from the sum above. The result will always be 7!

Suppose you start with the number 12.

12 + 12 = 24

24 + 5 = 29

29 + 12 = 41

41 – 3 = 38

38 ÷ 2 = 19

19 – 12 = 7

Go for It!

Are you still doubtful? Try this trick yourself. Then surprise your friends with it. You'll be in "seventh heaven" when you see the looks on their faces!

Eight's Great!

The number 8 is pretty neat. You'll see. Complete the 8s table that's started below.

1 × 8 = 8   (0 + 8 = 8)

2 × 8 = 16   (1 + 6 = 7)

3 × 8 = 24   (2 + 4 = 6)

4 × 8 = 32   (3 + 2 = 5)

Are you noticing anything yet?

Keep going.

5 × 8 = ___   (_____)

6 × 8 = ___   (_____) (_____)

7 × 8 = ___   (_____) (_____)

8 × 8 = ___   (_____) (_____)

What do you notice about the sum of the digits of each product? (Look in the parentheses.) Do they decrease in order?

Try multiplying 8 by a series of larger numbers, such as 33, 34, 35, and so on. (You'll want to use your calculator for this.) Does the same thing hold true for larger numbers?

Nine's Fine

Do you have trouble multiplying by 9? Well, you won't anymore. That's why this trick deserves a big hand!

The Nine Trick

Suppose you forget what 9 × 4 is. Just do this. Hold your hands out in front of you. Start with the little finger on your left hand. Count off four fingers. Bend down that finger. Now you have your answer! There are three fingers before the bent finger. There are six fingers after the bent finger. The answer is 36! (9 × 4 = 36)

Try it with other digits from 1 through 9. You'll never have trouble multiplying by 9 again.

If two's company and three's a crowd, what are four and five?

Nine!

Nine Each Time

Here's another 9 trick.

- Take a four-digit number.

- Now write the digits in reverse.

- Subtract the smaller number from the larger number.

- Add the digits of the answer.

- Then add the digits of that answer.

The answer will always be 9!

(Are you doubtful? Try it a few times.)

Suppose you pick the number 2,635.

2,635

5,362

5,362 – 2,653 = 2,709

2 + 7 + 0 + 9 = 18

1 + 8 = 9

Nifty Nine

More tricks with 9? You bet!

- Pick any number.
- Multiply by 9.
- Add the digits in the answer.

Did you get 9? If not, add the digits again. The answer will be 9 each time. It will work whether the number is large or small.

It All Adds Up . . .

Look closely at the times table for 9s. What do you notice?

$9 \times 1 = 9$

$9 \times 2 = 18$

$9 \times 3 = 27$

$9 \times 4 = 36$

$9 \times 5 = 45$

$9 \times 6 = 54$

$9 \times 7 = 63$

$9 \times 8 = 72$

$9 \times 9 = 81$

Choose a product from the times table for 9s. Now add any number from 1 through 9 to it. Add the digits of your answer until you get a single digit. You'll get the number you added!

Suppose you pick the number 74.

74

$74 \times 9 = 666$

$6 + 6 + 6 = 18$

$1 + 8 = 9$

Suppose you pick the number 437.

437

$437 \times 9 = 3,933$

$3 + 9 + 3 + 3 = 18$

$1 + 8 = 9$

Suppose you pick the number 54.

54

$54 + 3 = 57$

$5 + 7 = 12$

$1 + 2 = 3$

To the Nines!

Did you know that the expression "dressed to the nines" means very fashionably and elaborately dressed? "The nine" once symbolized being outstanding. Perhaps 9, being the largest single-digit number, symbolized the best. No one knows for sure. But here are a few more reasons 9 is tops!

Multiply

To multiply any number by 9:

$$9 \times 23{,}456$$

Place a 0 at the end of that number: 234,560

Subtract the original number: −23,456

And you'll have your answer: $9 \times 23{,}456 = 211{,}104$

Divide and Conquer

If a number is divisible by 9, the sum of the number's digits is 9.

(If the sum of the digits is greater than 9, add again until 9 is obtained.)

$$9 \overline{)\,40{,}743} \quad \frac{4{,}527}{}$$

4 + 5 + 2 + 7 = 18, and 1 + 8 = 9

$$9 \overline{)\,5{,}427} \quad \frac{603}{}$$

6 + 3 = 9

Number Madness

Any Number of Times

Do the expressions "back to square one" or "going around in circles" mean anything to you? Try this trick a few times. Choose a different number each time. What happens?

- Pick any number.
- Add 30 to it.
- Multiply the sum by 2.
- Subtract 4.
- Divide the answer by 2.
- Subtract 28.

23 Skidoo!

In your great-grandparents' time, "23 skidoo" meant *drop it* or *let's go*. With this trick, it's not so easy to get rid of 23.

- Choose any three-digit number.
- Add 25 to it.
- Multiply the sum by 2.
- Subtract 4.
- Divide the answer by 2.
- Subtract your three-digit number from this answer.
- Choose different three-digit numbers and repeat the process. It works over and over again.

Suppose you pick the number 8.

$$8$$
$$8 + 30 = 38$$
$$38 \times 2 = 76$$
$$76 - 4 = 72$$
$$72 \div 2 = 36$$
$$36 - 28 = 8$$

Suppose you pick the number 421.

$$421$$
$$421 + 25 = 446$$
$$446 \times 2 = 892$$
$$892 - 4 = 888$$
$$888 \div 2 = 444$$
$$444 - 421 = 23$$

Birthday Magic

Would you like to know someone's birthday? This trick works every time—as long as your math is correct. Just follow these directions.

Tell a friend to write down the month and date of his or her birthday. (Use numbers for the months, such as 1 for January, 2 for February, and so on.) Then tell your friend to do these things:

- Multiply the *month* number by 5.

- Add 6 to the product.

- Multiply the new answer by 4.

- Add 9 to this answer.

- Multiply the new answer by 5.

- Add the day of the month for the birthday to this answer.

Now ask your friend what the last answer is. *Subtract 165 from that number.* Look at the last two digits. They form the *day* of the month for your friend's birthday. The first one or two digits will be the *month* number.

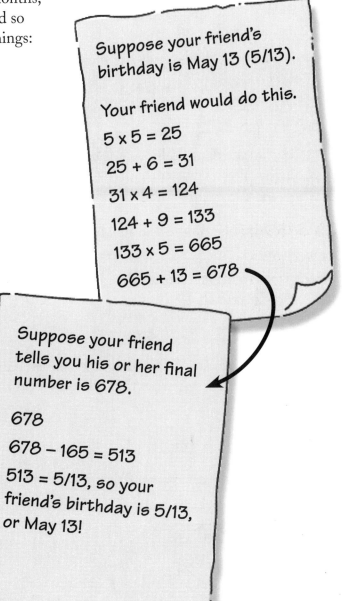

Suppose your friend's birthday is May 13 (5/13).

Your friend would do this.

5 x 5 = 25

25 + 6 = 31

31 x 4 = 124

124 + 9 = 133

133 x 5 = 665

665 + 13 = 678

Suppose your friend tells you his or her final number is 678.

678

678 – 165 = 513

513 = 5/13, so your friend's birthday is 5/13, or May 13!

Nothing "Phone-y" Here

Can you guess someone's birth year from a phone number?
You sure can. Here's how.

Give someone the following directions:

- Write down the last four digits of your phone number.

- Now take those digits and write them in another order.

- Subtract the smaller number from the larger number.

- Add up all the digits individually and keep adding until you get a single digit.

- Add 16 to the result.

- Add this number to the year in which you were born.

- Tell what your final number is.

Suppose the last four digits of the phone number are 0450.

5004
5004 − 0450 = 4554
4 + 5 + 5 + 4 = 18
1 + 8 = 9
9 + 16 = 25
25 + 1994 = 2019
2019 − 25 = 1994
ANSWER: Your friend's birth year is 1994.

What you do:

Take that last number and subtract 25 from that number to get the birth year.

For Ages and Ages . . .

Here's another way to figure out a person's age.

Give these directions to the person:

- Take your present age and add it to your age next year.

- Now multiply that sum by 5.

- Add the last digit of your year of birth.

- Now subtract 5.

The number formed by the two *left*-most digits is the person's age.

Use these spaces to try out the trick on someone in your family.

Suppose someone is 20 years old, born in 1986.

This is what the person would do.

20 + 21 = 41

41 × 5 = 205

205 + 6 = 211

211 − 5 = 206

Now you can look at the two left-most digits to get that person's age: 20.

Birthday Math

Riddle: What is it that, after you take away the whole, some still remains? (See page 154 for the answer.)

- Write the year of your birth.
- Double it.
- Add 5.
- Multiply by 50.
- Add your age.
- Add 365.
- Subtract 615.

The first four digits will always be the year of your birth. The last two digits will always be your age.

Can't Be Fooled

Here's another way to guess a person's age.

- Ask a person to "secretly" multiply his or her age by 3.
- Tell the person to add 6 to that number.
- Then the person should divide that sum by 3 and tell you the answer.
- If you secretly subtract 2 from the person's answer, the result will be the person's true age.

Suppose you were born in 1994.

1994 + 1994 = 3988
3988 + 5 = 3993
3993 x 50 = 199,650
199,650 + 12 = 199,662
199,662 + 365 = 200,027
200,027 − 615 = 199,412

Example:

9 (age) x 3 = 27
27 + 6 = 33
33 ÷ 3 = 11
11 − 2 = 9

It All Adds Up—*Fast!*

Tell a friend that you can add in "lightning speed." To prove your claim, turn to any month on a calendar. Use the calendar month on this page for practice.

Tell your friend:

- Choose a full week of 7 days. It can be any week of any month as long as it has 7 days.

- Now add the numbers in that week. But don't tell me the sum. Just tell me the number of the first day of the week, and I'll get the sum, too.

  When your friend tells you the first day, you'll have the answer before your friend can add up the numbers to get the sum.

S	M	T	W	TH	F	S
						1
2	3	4	5	6	7	8
9	10	11	12	13	14	15
16	17	18	19	20	21	22
23	24	25	26	27	28	29
30	31					

Race to the Finish . . .

Suppose your friend chooses the week that begins on Sunday, the 2nd.

- Your friend says, "I'm choosing the week starting on the 2nd." You say: "Then your sum is 35"—before your friend can finish adding up the days: 2 + 3 + 4 + 5 + 6 + 7 + 8 = 35.

- How did you do that? The trick is to add 3 to the first day of the week. Then multiply the sum by 7. For example: 2 + 3 = 5. 5 x 7 = 35.

Suppose your friend chooses the week beginning with Sunday, the 9th.

- Do the following: 9 + 3 = 12. 12 x 7 = 84.

- Meanwhile, your friend is doing this: 9 + 10 + 11 + 12 + 13 + 14 + 15 = 84.

- You will be able to arrive at the answer faster than your friend can.

- Try it for the week beginning on Sunday, the 16th. Who finishes first?

It's a Date

Do you have a calendar? Good. Use it for some neat tricks.

The Square Deal

- Tell your friends to choose a square on the calendar. The square must have nine numbers.

- Tell your friends not to show you the square, but only to tell you the middle number:

14	15	16
21	22	23
28	29	30

The middle number in the example above is 22.

S	M	T	W	TH	F	S
			1	2	3	4
5	6	7	8	9	10	11
12	13	14	15	16	17	18
19	20	21	22	23	24	25
26	27	28	29	30	31	

- Now tell your friends to add up the nine numbers—first, row by row; then, together:

$$
\begin{array}{rcl}
14 + 15 + 16 &=& 63 \\
21 + 22 + 23 &=& 66 \\
28 + 29 + 30 &=& \underline{+69} \\
& & 198
\end{array}
$$

- While your friends are slaving away, you can give them their answer! How? Just multiply their middle number by nine: **22 x 9 = 198**. It works every time!

Double Cross

- Draw a rule around four boxes on a calendar. Add the numbers diagonally. Look at the two sums you get. What do you notice? Will it work every time? Check it out.

S	M	T	W	TH	F	S
				1	2	3	4
5	6	7	8	9	10	11
12	13	14	15	16	17	18
19	20	21	22	23	24	25
26	27	28	29	30	31	

9   10
16   17

9 + 17 = 26
16 + 10 = 26

Magic Four

- Draw a box around any four dates on a calendar.

- Add up the four numbers. **(Example: 9 + 10 + 17 + 16 = 52)**

- Divide the number by 4. **(52 ÷ 4 = 13)**

- Subtract 4. **(13 − 4 = 9)**

- Compare your answer with the number at the top left corner of your box. It matches!

- Choose 4 new numbers and go through the same steps. It works each time—*four*-tunately!

Some months have 31 days, and some have 30 days. How many months have 28 days?

All of them.

Happy Birth(Day)!

Do you know the day of the week on which you were born? Here's a way to find out.

Suppose you were born May 13, 1997.

1. Write the last two digits of the year: 97

2. Divide that number by 4. Don't count the remainder. Write the answer.

$$\overset{24r1}{4\overline{)97}}$$ Use this number: 24

3. Look at the chart below and write the number that goes with your birth month.

January 1
February 4
March 4
April 0
May 2
June 5
July 0
August 3
September 6
October 1
November 4
December 6

Example: 2

4. Write the day of the month for your birthday.
   Example: 13

5. Add the answers to steps 1 through 4:

   ```
      97
      24
       2
    +13
    ___
     136
   ```

6. Divide by 7.

$$\overset{19r3}{7\overline{)136}}$$

Suppose you were born
May 13, 1997.

Step 1: 97

Step 2: 97 ÷ 4 = 24r1
(Use 24.)

Step 3: 2

Step 4: 13

Step 5:
97 + 24 + 2 + 13 = 136

Step 6:
136 ÷ 7 = 19r3

7. Find the *remainder* in the chart below. It tells you the day of the week on which you were born. If you were born on May 13, 1997, you were born on a Tuesday.

Sunday 1
Monday 2
Tuesday 3
Wednesday 4
Thursday 5
Friday 6
Saturday 0

Step 7:
3 is the remainder

3 on the chart is Tuesday!

Days of Your Life

Make a fist to remember the days in each month. Look at your fist and say the months in order. Point to the knuckle on your little finger. That's January. The space between is February. The next knuckle is March. Keep going to July. Then go back to the little knuckle for "August" and keep going. All the "knuckle months" have 31 days. The in-betweens have only 30, except for February, of course. It has 28 days—or 29 when it is a leap year.

Fun Fact

Happy New Year

A year is the time it takes for the Earth to revolve around the Sun once. A calendar year is 365 days. A cosmic year is the amount of time it takes the Sun to revolve around the center of the Milky Way. A cosmic year is about 225 million years.

Year by Year

Here are some common ways to group years:

Olympiad	4 years
Decade	10 years
Score	20 years
Century	100 years
Millennium	1,000 years

Magic Squares

Magic squares have been used for thousands of years. According to an old Chinese legend, there lived a very special tortoise. It had a very strange design of numbers on its shell. Shown here are the numbers as they appeared on the shell. Can you guess what is so special about the way the numbers are arranged?

Add the numbers in each row, column, and diagonal. Now you know. Each sum is 15. A *magic square* is a square of numbers that add up to the same number—across, down, and diagonally. That number is the square's *magic number*.

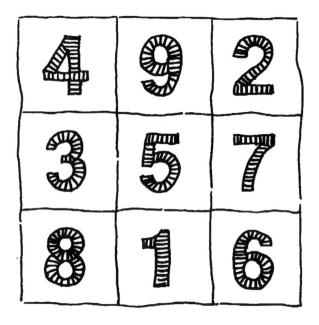

The Winning Square

You can play "Magic Square Tic-Tac-Toe." Here's how. Take turns writing the numbers 1 through 9 in the spaces. The first player to complete a row that adds up to 15 is the winner.

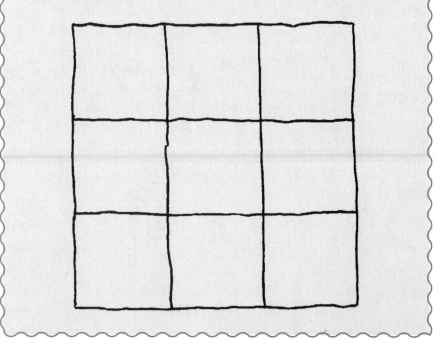

A Spin on Magic Squares

Try making up your own magic squares. Draw a square with three rows across and down. Write the numbers 1 through 9 in the nine spaces. The trick is to arrange the numbers so that the numbers in each row, column, and diagonal add up to 15!

Hint: Turn the original square on its left side, like this.

Now copy the top row into an empty square. Fill in the rest to get a new magic square.

Keep Spinning . . .

Turn the original square to the left, to the right, upside down. Hold it up to a mirror. How many new magic squares can you make? Check to be sure the sum of the numbers in each row, column, and diagonal is 15.

Is This Square "Four" Real?

This magic square appeared in a painting done in 1514 by German artist Albrecht Dürer. Can you complete it?

(Hint: First figure out what the magic number is. Then fill in the empty spaces.)

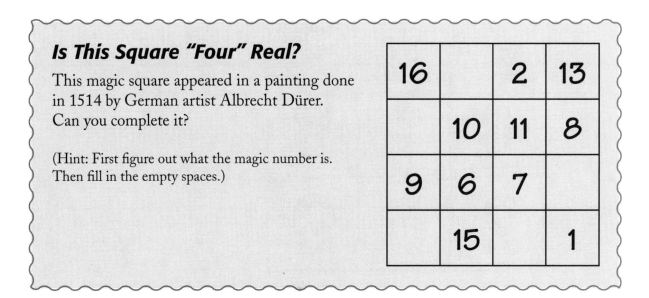

16		2	13
	10	11	8
9	6	7	
	15		1

"Sum" Square

Look at the diagonal line below. Notice that it passes through boxes that total 13.
(3 + 1 + 9)

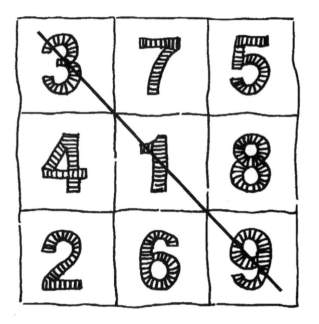

It's your turn. What's the greatest total you can make by drawing one straight line in any direction? (Use a ruler.) See page 154 for the answer.

Ah—Googol!

Is this a computer search engine? Is this baby talk? No. But a young person invented the math term *googol*. A googol is the name given to one of the greatest numbers imaginable. A googol is 1 followed by 100 zeros.

In the early 1900s, American mathematician Edward Kasner was thinking about very large numbers. His 9-year-old nephew suggested the name *googol*. Then he came up with the name for an even larger number. The term *googolplex* is 1 followed by 10 to the power of a googol of zeroes, or 1 followed by 10,000 zeroes. Some sum, huh?

Imagine numbers without zero. How does having zero change things?

Hint: In columns of numbers, how would you keep your tens, hundreds, and thousands columns straight?

Can you imagine a number that has endless numbers of zeros after it? The idea that numbers go on forever is expressed by the word *infinity*. Infinity is not a real number. It's just the idea that numbers can go on forever. Here is what the symbol for infinity looks like: ∞

This is a googol:
10,000,000,000,000,000,000,000,000,000,000,000,
000,000,000,000,000,000,000,000,000,000,000,000,
000,000,000,000,000,000,000,000,000,000

0	zero
1	one
10	ten
100	one hundred
1,000	one thousand
100,000	one hundred thousand
1,000,000	one million
1,000,000,000	one billion
1,000,000,000,000	one trillion

Animal Planet

- The sperm whale has the largest animal brain. It weighs about 20 pounds.

- One beehive can house 80,000 bees at a time.

- The giraffe has only 7 neck bones— just like a person! A giraffe's tongue can measure 21 inches.

- The average elephant eats 250 pounds of plants a day and drinks 50 gallons of water!

- The Asian mouse deer is 9 inches tall.

- For every person in the world, there are 200 million insects.

- The blue whale is the largest animal that ever lived. It can grow to be 100 feet long and weigh up to 150 tons! This is as much as 23 elephants, or 1,800 men.

- An electric eel can produce a shock of 600 volts. That's enough to knock a horse off its feet (or hooves, as the case may be).

- Hummingbirds flap their wings between 50 and 70 times a second!

- Some ducks can fly as far as 332 miles a day.

- A cat has 32 muscles in each ear.

- Starfish have 8 eyes—one at the end of each leg.

- A duck has 3 eyelids.

- Female lions do 90 percent of the hunting.

- An ostrich's egg weighs $3\frac{1}{2}$ pounds.

- A kangaroo can jump 45 feet.

- Cows have 4 stomachs.

Activity:

Make up three math problems based on any of the above data. Trade with a partner, and solve each other's problems.

Aren't You Special?

- If all the blood vessels in your body were laid end to end, they would reach about 60,000 miles. That's enough to go around the world twice.

- In one day, your heart beats 100,000 times.

- You have about 650 muscles in your body and 206 bones.

- When you sneeze, air goes through your nose at 100 mph.

- Your body is about 75 percent water. And your brain is 80 percent water!

- Your tongue has 3,000 taste buds.

- The smallest human bone is in the ear. The stirrup bone measures 0.1 inch long.

- The average person has 6 pounds of skin.

- The largest human bone is the thighbone, or *femur*. In a 6-foot-tall person, the femur would be 20 inches long. The femur is the strongest bone, too—and it's hollow!

- When you smile, you use 17 muscles. When you frown, you use more than 40!

- Your fingernails grow almost four times as fast as your toenails.

- You blink your eyes more than 10,000,000 times a year.

- Half your body's red blood cells are replaced every 7 days.

- For humans, the normal pulse is 70 heartbeats per minute. (Elephants have a slower pulse of 27 and for a canary it is 1,000!)

- It takes food 7 seconds to go from the mouth to the stomach by way of the esophagus.

Activity:

Make up three math problems based on any of the above data. Trade with a partner, and solve each other's problems.

It Figures

Let your imagination run wild. How many funny cartoons can you create from single digits?

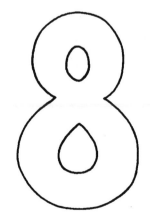

Mental Math:
Mind Benders and More

Just imagine how different your life would be
without math. How would you keep score in
a ball game? How would you follow a recipe?
How would you count sheep to fall asleep?
In this section, you'll be figuring out a mini-
mystery, flexing your mental muscles with some
brainteasers, and putting your creativity to the
test in a number of ways.

Be Creative!

We all know that 2 + 2 = 4. That's easy. But can you think of situations in which 2 + 2 does not equal 4?

Have fun with your answers! (A few ideas are on page 154, but don't peek!)

Examples: 2 rabbits + 2 rabbits = hundreds of rabbits

2 singers + 2 singers = 1 quartet

Can you think of other crazy equations?

Examples: 1 + 1 = 100 (one 50 + one 50 = 100)

5 + 5 = 1 (5 players + 5 players = 1 basketball game)

Any other ideas?

Seeing Things a "Number" of Ways

Here are some things that come in threes. Can you find more?

Examples: singers in a TRIO

wheels on a tricycle

angles in a triangle

blind mice

little pigs

Here is a fresh challenge for you—things that come in pairs. You can write or draw your answers.

Examples: salt and pepper

cup and saucer

There are more ideas on page 154, but don't peek!

And the Number is . . . 395!

This doesn't happen often. You're going to start out with the correct answer. But then you'll have to finish with it, too.

For each clue below, write the number that fits. Then add up all your numbers. If you get every clue right, your total should be 395! See page 154 for the clue answers.

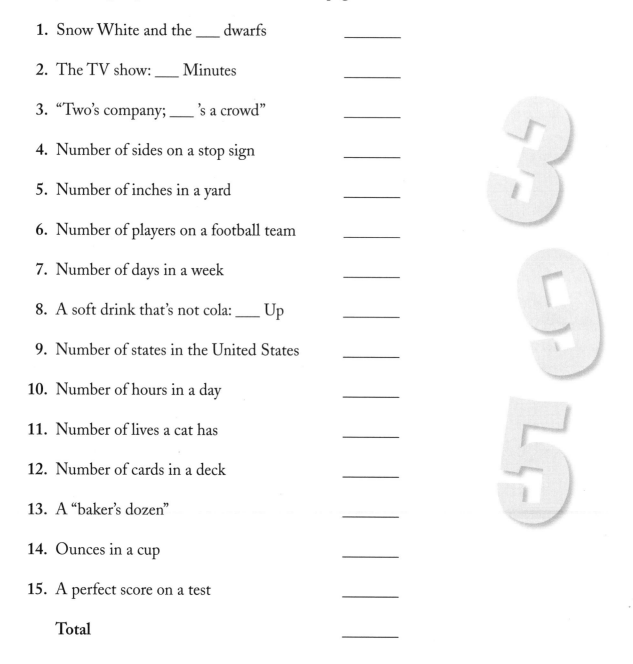

1. Snow White and the ___ dwarfs   _____

2. The TV show: ___ Minutes   _____

3. "Two's company; ___'s a crowd"   _____

4. Number of sides on a stop sign   _____

5. Number of inches in a yard   _____

6. Number of players on a football team   _____

7. Number of days in a week   _____

8. A soft drink that's not cola: ___ Up   _____

9. Number of states in the United States   _____

10. Number of hours in a day   _____

11. Number of lives a cat has   _____

12. Number of cards in a deck   _____

13. A "baker's dozen"   _____

14. Ounces in a cup   _____

15. A perfect score on a test   _____

    Total   _____

Brain Teasers

Are you up for a challenge? Good.
If you get stuck, you'll find the answers on page 154.

1. *Weighty Question*
Which weighs more—a pound of feathers or a pound of lead?

2. *Two Tricksters*
Two people meet at the bus stop. One looks at her watch and says, "Where I live, every day has 23 hours in it." The other person says, "Well, where I live, every week has six days in it." Both people are correct. How can that be?

3. *On the Move*
If 10 caterpillars take 10 minutes to crawl 10 feet, how long would it take 20 caterpillars to crawl 10 feet?

4. *It All Adds Up*
You have two coins. Added together, they equal 55 cents, but one is not a nickel. How is that possible?

5. *What a Bunch!*
If there are six bananas and you take away four, how many bananas do you have?

6. *Shop Talk*
If one worker in a butcher shop is 6' 3" tall, what does he weigh?

Riddle
A dime and a quarter stood at the edge of a cliff. The dime leaned over and fell off. Why didn't the quarter?

7. *Divide and Conquer*
What do you get if you add 10 to one-half of 50?

8. *This One's "Four" You*
How many times can you subtract 4 from 62—and what do you get?

9. *Stay on Track*
If a train is 1 mile long and is traveling at 1 mile per minute, how long will it take the train to go through a tunnel that is 1 mile long?

10. *Chew on This*
There are red, yellow, and blue gumballs in gumball machine. All but four are red; all but four are yellow; and all but four are blue. How many gumballs are in the gumball machine all together?

The Case of "Finders Keepers"

The girl caught her brother in a bald-faced lie. How did she know he was lying?

If you get stumped, the answer is on page 154.

Math Works:
Music, Language, Art, History

What does math have to do with music or poetry? How do artists use math? What do history buffs know about math? What kind of wordplay involves math? You'll find the answers to these questions and more in this section. Just proceed at your own pace, "measure for measure."

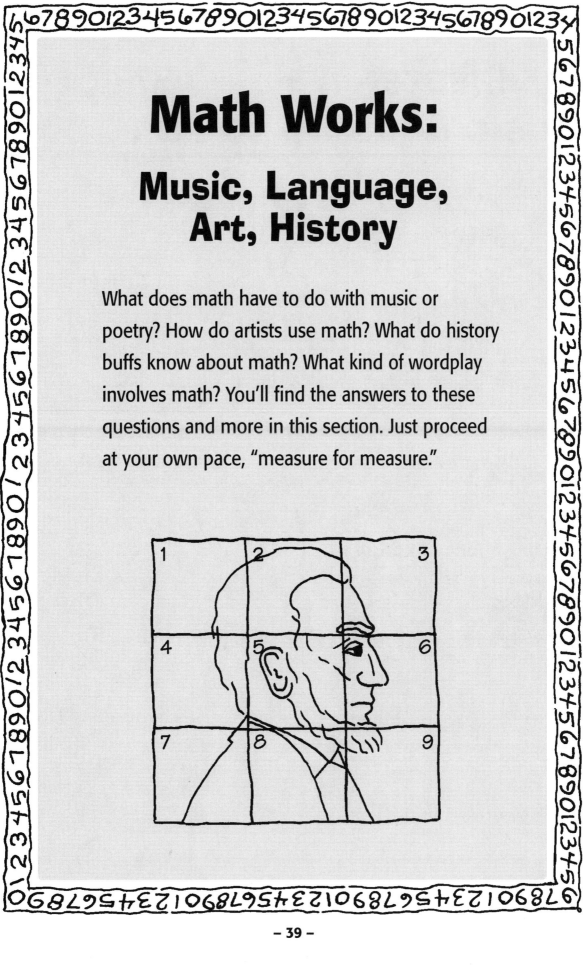

Take Note: Music Adds Up to Fun

When it comes to music, do you know the score? People who write music write in notes. Every note makes a certain sound. It also lasts a certain length of time. If you can count to four, you can see how notes add up.

The Long and the Short of It

Every note has a value. The value comes in beats or counts. Here's how it works for a piece of music written in 4/4 time.

This is a **whole note**. A whole note lasts for four counts. (For practice, have someone count to four as you sing one lone note.)

This is a **half note**. Its value is two counts. (Have someone count 1, 2 as you sing a note.)

This is a **quarter note**. Its value is one count.

This is an **eighth note**. Its value is half a count. (Sing eight short notes as a friend counts to four: LA-LA-LA-LA-LA-LA-LA-LA.)

1   2   3   4

For Good Measure

Composers take notes of different lengths and put them together. Long and short notes are put into groups called measures. Each measure contains notes.

Put together your own musical groups. Remember that in 4/4 time, each group of notes must add up to four. You can use whole notes, half notes, quarter notes, and eighth notes.

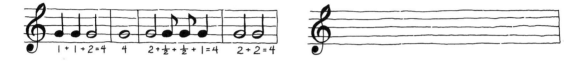

Sound Idea

It's important to know how long a note lasts. But it's also important to know what sound a note makes. That's why notes are written on lines called the musical staff. The placement of the notes on the lines tells their sounds. The higher a note is on the staff, the higher its sound.

Here are the different notes and their sounds. The notes on the lines are E-G-B-D-F (**E**very **G**ood **B**oy **D**oes **F**ine). The notes in the spaces are F-A-C-E.

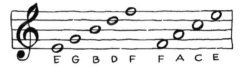

Some Fun

These jokes add up to fun if you can figure out the missing words. Look at the musical staffs for the answers. The "name" of the notes spells out each missing word. Answers are on page 154.

1. Is it _____ luck if a black cat follows you?
   Only if you're a mouse!

2. Why are oysters lazy?
   They are always found in _____s.

3. What's stranger than a talking dog?
   A spelling _____.

4. When isn't it a good idea to crack up?
   When you're an _____.

5. What number increases each year?
   Your _____.

Be a Band "Liter"

Are you looking for a sound idea? Then hop aboard the musical bandwagon. People have been making—and playing—simple instruments for years. You can join the fun. Try different kinds. Then you and your friends can strike up the band.

Water Bells

Collect six same-sized bottles. Fill one with 1.5 liters of water. Fill another with 1.25 liters of water, the next with 1 liter, then .75, .5, and .25. Be sure each bottle has a different amount of water. Add food coloring to each bottle for a pretty effect. Line up the bottles in order of water level. Then use a metal spoon to tap out a colorful tune.

Horns of Plenty

Collect large bottles. Measure out different amounts of water into each bottle. Each horn player chooses a bottle and blows air across the top of the hole in the bottle.

Drum

Take an empty coffee can. Cut out a circle from cooking parchment paper large enough to cover the top of the can. Use a rubber band to keep the paper in place. Use two pencils to drum your beats.

Shakers

Fill empty food cans with dry beans or rice to make shakers. You can also use cardboard tubes from toilet paper rolls. Cover one end with wax paper and a rubber band, add rice, and then cover the other end.

Bag It

Fill up a paper lunch bag with air. Hold the bag with the top under your arm. Now slap the bag gently with your hand. Try to work on different rhythms. Having friends do the same with different-sized bags to get different sounds.

Fibonacci's Secret

Look closely at these numbers. Do you see a pattern?

0 1 1 2 3 5 8 13 21

Each number is the sum of the two preceding it.

(For example: 1 + 2 = 3, 2 + 3 = 5, and so on.)

Leonardo Fibonacci, a mathematician who lived around 1200, noted this pattern. What's more, Fibonacci numbers have a lot to do with creating harmonious sounds. You'll find them in most songs and lyrics. Think of a tune you know. Count the musical notes in each line. Do you get a Fibonacci number?

Fibonacci numbers appear as patterns in nature, too. Pine cones, asparagus tip, and pineapple florets are arranged in sets of spirals that are consecutive Fibonacci numbers.

Sumsational Wordplay

Can you think of other math words? Try writing them to show their meanings.

Say What?

Can you guess these three expressions? If you get stumped, see page 154 for the answers.

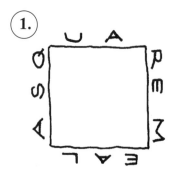

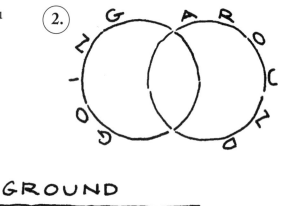

see page 154 for the answers.

Word

What math meanings do these words have? What other meanings do they have?

odd	even	prime	digit	count	figure	table
times	plot	ruler	round	measure	foot	pound
angle	line	product	positive	negative		

Palindromes

Look at these words:

mom   dad   sees   eve   radar   noon   peep

Do you notice anything unusual? They each read the same backward and forward. Words that do so are called *palindromes*. Here are whole-sentence palindromes:

Madam, I'm Adam.

A man. A plan. A canal: Panama!

Numbers can be palindromes, too. Here are a few examples:

707   242   696   939   1221

Go Digital

Think of a digital watch face. How many palindromes would appear during the course of a single day? For example: 1:01, 1:11, 1:21, and so on. See page 154 for the answer.

Create Your Own Palindromes

Here's a neat little trick.

- First, write down any three-digit number.

- Then make a new number by reversing its digits.

- Add the two numbers.

- Keep reversing and adding until you get a palindrome.

Suppose you pick the number 527.

527

725

527 + 725 = 1252

1252 + 2521 = 3773

Rhyme Time

If you say poems aloud, you will hear their special rhythms. Tap your fingers in time to the beats you hear. Try these funny limericks:

There once was an old man with a beard,

Who said, "It is just as I feared!—

Two owls and a hen,

Four larks and a wren,

Have all built their nests in my beard!"

There was a young lady of Kent,

Whose nose was most awfully bent.

One day, I suppose,

She followed her nose,

For no one knew which way she went.

Limerick Lingo

A *limerick* is a short, silly poem of five lines. A limerick follows these rules:

- Lines 1, 2, and 5 rhyme.

- Lines 1, 2, and 5 have eight to ten beats.

- Lines 3 and 4 rhyme.

- Lines 3 and 4 have five to seven beats.

Are you ready to give it a try? First, fill in the missing words from the limerick below. Then write your own!

There once was a barber named Stu

Who worked very hard at the _____

He was very brave

To give the lion a _____

And give the brown bear a shampoo!

Fun Fact

Measure for Measure

Did you know that poets speak of meters and measures? They do. Poets write lines of verse that are measured in terms of "metrical feet." Often, poetry is made up of measures of two syllables each, with the accent on the second syllable. Here is an example from Shakespeare: "To be / or not / to be".

_____

_____

_____

_____

_____

Poetry: And the Beat Goes On . . .

If you can count, you can write some interesting poems.

Haiku

A haiku is a three-line poem. Each line has a certain number of beats, or syllables.

Example:	**Best Friends**
Line One—5 syllables	*When I first met you*
Line Two—7 syllables	*It was like seeing myself.*
Line Three—5 syllables	*You are my mirror image.*

Tanka

A tanka poem is longer than a haiku. It is five lines long. The first three lines have the same number of syllables as the first three lines of a haiku. The last two lines each have seven syllables.

Example:	**Surprise!**
Line One—5 syllables	*It is your birthday.*
Line Two—7 syllables	*I brought you a cuddly pup*
Line Three—5 syllables	*To love and cherish.*
Line Four—7 syllables	*I wrapped it up in ribbons.*
Line Five—7 syllables	*And left it on your doorstep.*

Heartbeats

What things matter to you? Write your own haiku and tanka in the spaces.

Haiku Title: _____

Line 1: _____

Line 2: _____

Line 3: _____

Tanka Title: _____

Line 1: _____

Line 2: _____

Line 3: _____

Line 4: _____

Line 5: _____

Quick at the Draw!

Here's a neat way to copy pictures. You can make your pictures large or small.
All you need to do a scale drawing is a pencil and some graph paper:

1. Start with a picture.

2. Draw squares on
   top of the picture.

3. Make another set of
   squares exactly the
   same size.

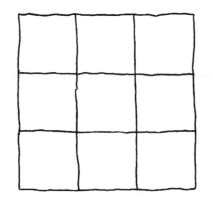

4. Copy the picture onto your squares. Copy the squares one by one. Start with the top left square. Then do the square next to it. Keep going until you finish line one. Do line two, and so on. When you finish all the squares, your picture is done.

Now that you know the basics, you can have some fun. Do you want a jumbo picture? Then make a set of bigger squares. Copy your picture again. You will be making the same picture, but the *scale* will be larger.

Do you want a teeny, tiny picture? Then make your second set of squares very small.

Try changing the squares into *rectangles*. You can use short, fat rectangles or tall, skinny rectangles. What kind of crazy pictures did you get?

Ready, Get Set, Draw!

Find a picture you would like to copy. Use graph paper or draw your own squares. How many ways can you copy the picture?

Scaling New Heights

Did you know that the heads that are carved on Mount Rushmore are 75 times the size of a human head? Artists have a way of making things larger or smaller than real life. It's called *scale drawing*. Here's how you do it.

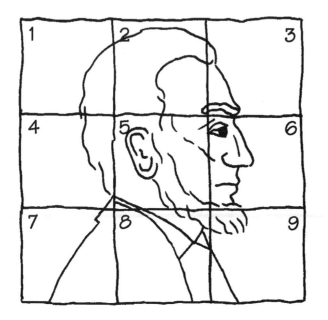

Look at the part of the picture in Box 1. Copy that shape into Box A. Now copy the shape from Box 2 into Box B. Copy the shapes box by box to make the picture larger.

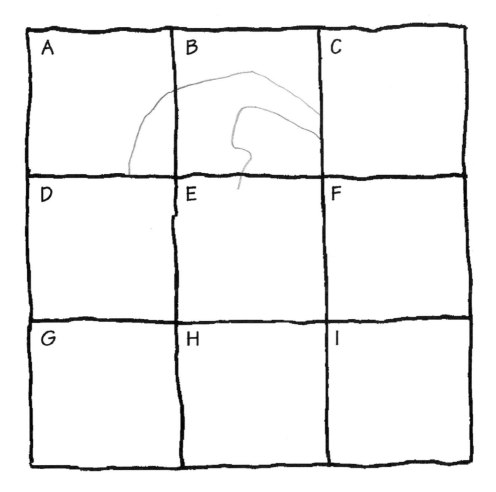

To make the picture smaller, copy the shape from Box 1 into Box J. Then copy the shape from Box 2 into Box K. Again, keep going. When you're done, you'll have a tiny face.

History: Measure for Measure

One Cubit at a Time

In earliest times, people probably used parts of their bodies to describe lengths and quantities. But the first unit of measurement ever recorded was the cubit. A cubit was the length of a forearm from the elbow to the fingertip of the middle finger.

Best Foot Forward

Greeks and Romans had an "Olympic cubit," which was about 18 inches. Two-thirds of this cubit became the first foot.

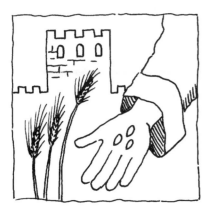

Inch by Inch

The Greeks divided the foot into 12 "thumbnail" measures. Then King Edward II of England, in the fourteenth century, decreed that the inch was the length of three barleycorns, round and dry.

In Good Measure

People's occupations had a lot to do with measurements they developed and used. The English were sailors, so they developed a unit to measure the depth of water. This was called the fathom. The word fathom meant "outstretched arms." One fathom equaled the length across a man's outstretched arms (about 6 feet).

The English were also cloth merchants. So they created the yard to measure cloth. A yard was equal to half of a fathom, or the distance from the middle of the chest to the fingertip of an outstretched arm. Suppose one merchant's arm was shorter than another's? Then he'd sell a shorter yard of material!

The Standard Yard

To regulate trade, you need uniformity in measures. The English kings wrote laws to establish standards. King Henry I decreed that the lawful yard was the distance from the point of his nose to the end of his thumb. Later, King Henry VII overruled him. He decreed that the standard yard measured three feet and had the measure marked on a bronze yard bar.

Knot So Fast!

Sailors measure a ship's speed through water in knots. The word *knot* comes from the fact that sailors actually tied knots at regular intervals to a log. (The knots were made about every 47 feet.) A sailor threw the log overboard and counted the number of knots slipping through his fingers in one minute (timed with a sandglass). If the seaman counted 5 knots, the ship was said to be traveling at 5 knots (5 nautical miles per hour).

Fun Fact

Are You Worth Your Weight in Gold?

The "carat" is used to show the weight of jewels. The Arabs used a karob bean, or carat, to weigh against gold. That's how we got the "K" that is used in gold weight. A carat was once 4 grains. Now it is 3,086 grains (a grain = 0.0022085 ounce).

Go Figure . . .

A knot equals 1.15 miles per hour. To change from miles per hour to knots, you divide by 1.15. So 38 miles per hour is the same as about 33 knots. See the example.

Suppose you want to change from knots to miles per hour. Then you'd *multiply* by 1.15. (Round to the nearest whole number.)

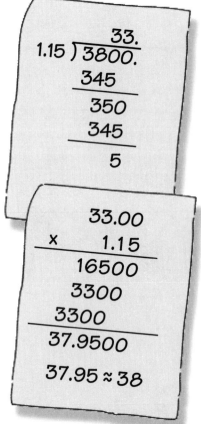

So Long, Furlongs

The English were farmers, too. So they developed the furlong, which was the length of a furrow, or track, plowed by a farmer.

Hello, Rodmen

In the sixteenth century, the length of a *rod* was determined by lining up 16 men as they left church on Sunday morning! Today we don't use rods. Instead, we say 1 furlong = 660 feet, or 8 furlongs = 1 mi.

Meet the Meter

During the French Revolution, scientists invented a new system of measurement. They called it the metric system. Metrics is a decimal system based on permanent standards—not king's orders! The basic unit of length is the meter. A meter is exactly one ten-millionth of the distance from the Earth's equator to either pole.

Space-Age Measures

Today, scientists use incredibly small and large measurements. For example, the angstrom measures 264-millionths of an inch! A light year is the distance a beam of light covers in one calendar year—that's approximately six trillion miles!

American Linear System

12 inches	1 foot
3 feet	1 yard
2 yards	1 fathom
$5\frac{1}{2}$ yards	1 rod
220 yards	1 furlong
1,760 yards	1 mile

Metric System

10 millimeters	1 centimeter
10 centimeters	1 decimeter
10 decimeters	1 meter
10 meters	1 dekameter
1,000 meters	1 kilometer

Peter Piper Picked a Peck of Pickled Peppers . . .

How about . . . ?

A bale of cotton = 500 pounds

A hand of bananas = a small bunch

A bolt of cloth = about 40 yards

A baker's dozen = 13

A ream of paper = 500 sheets

A fortnight = 2 weeks

A drum of oil = 50–55 gallons

A peck = 8 quarts

Give the Gray Mare a Hand

Today a "hand" is 4 inches and is used to measure horses (from the ground to the horse's shoulders).

Who's Got the Power?

The brightness of an electric light is measure in *candlepower*. The measure *manpower* equals what the average person can lift 1 foot high in 1 second, or 55 pounds. A workhorse can lift 550 pounds 1 foot in the air in 1 second—that is 1 *horsepower*. Engines are measured in horsepower. A 50-horsepower engine can do the work of 50 horses.

Fun Fact

Way to Go!

Light travels through space at 186,000 miles per second. The fastest jet plane goes about 2,000 mph. The fastest car travels 205 mph. A cheetah, the fastest animal, moves 70 mph. A person can move 27.8 mph, whereas a snail goes 0.03 mph.

They Made Their Mark

People have been dividing things into units for ages. Here are four basic units:

Sexagesimal: Time is measured in 60s. There are 60 seconds in a minute, 60 minutes in an hour. The Babylonians were the first to use units of 60.

Decimal: The Chinese and Egyptians were the first to use decimals, which are units of 10. The metric system is based on decimals, as is the Dewey Decimal System of arranging library books.

Duodecimal: There are 12 inches in a foot, 12 months in a year, 12 in a dozen. The Romans used units of 12.

Binary: Hindus first divided things into halves, quarters, and eighths.

* If 4 pecks = 1 bushel, then "a bushel and a peck" is equal to how many bushels? (Answer on page 154.)

How Do You Measure Up?

Your wrist is twice as big around as your thumb. At least, that's the way it is with most people. Measure and see. Get a piece of string about 3 feet long. Put one end of it around the base of our thumb. Hold the string at the meeting place. Then take the string from your thumb and *double* the length of string. Now try this length around your wrist. Does it fit?

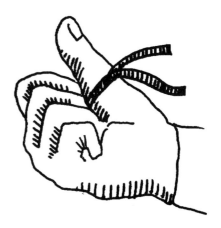

Double the string again. What part of you is twice as big around as your wrist? For most people, it's their neck.

Keep stringing along. Double the string again. Can you find a place that is twice as big as your neck?

All Thumbs

Trace your footprint on a piece of paper. Then use your thumb to measure your foot. This picture shows how to make off thumb widths.

Is your foot 12 thumbs long? Years ago, Romans used their thumbs and feet to measure things. Today, we still do as the Romans did. We divide our "foot" into 12 parts. The Romans called a thumb's width a *unica*. Our word inch comes from *unica*.

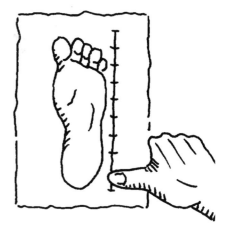

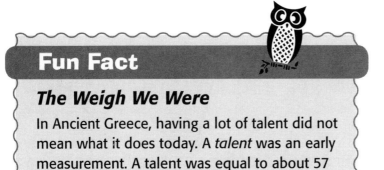

Fun Fact

The Weigh We Were

In Ancient Greece, having a lot of talent did not mean what it does today. A *talent* was an early measurement. A talent was equal to about 57 pounds. The *girth* is the measure around your stomach. Fishing line was measured in girths.

Is Seeing Believing?

Sometimes your eyes play tricks on you. Treat yourself to the "tricks" of optical illusions.

Line Up!

Not all things are as they seem. Use a ruler to measure the lines.

Which line is longer—A or B?

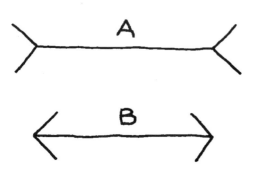

Which line is longer—DC or EF?

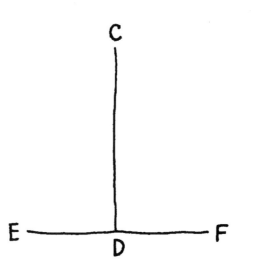

Which line is longer—GH or HI?

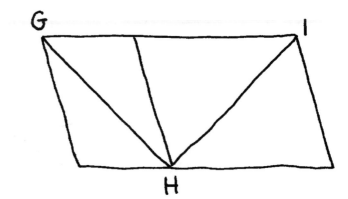

How Do You See It?

Is the center sticking out or back?

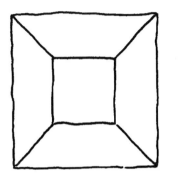

Left to right, or right to left?

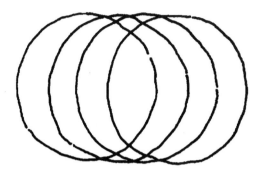

Is the gray portion the inside or the outside?

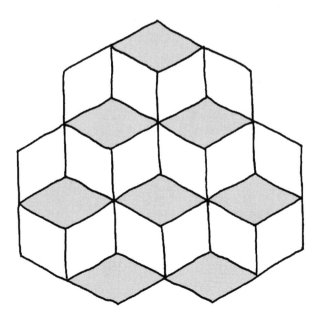

Six or seven cubes?

Sign on and Be Counted

Some people use American Sign Language to express numbers. If you learn these signs, you will be able to figure out some math problems. Answers are on page 154.

ASL Signs for the Numbers 1–10

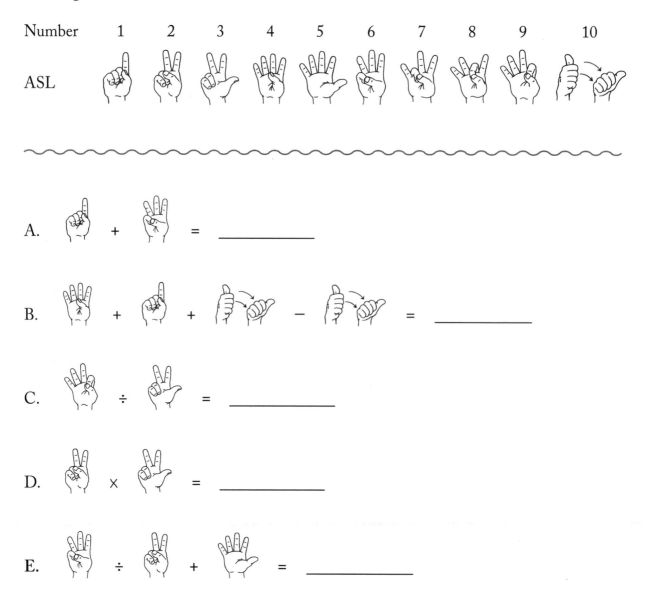

Math Matters:
Fun Fare

After you've read this section, you'll be ready for some real undercover work. You'll crack secret codes and unlock hidden messages. You'll solve puzzles, get the lowdown on Roman numerals, figure your worth, and make your own fortune-teller. Then, finally, you'll match wits (or lose them) when you take the Test of Champions.

It's ~~Greek~~ Roman to Me

Do Roman numerals look like a secret code? To break the code, all you need to know are seven symbols:

I	=	1
V	=	5
X	=	10
L	=	50
C	=	100
D	=	500
M	=	1,000

Just **add** the value of these symbols in various combinations to get most numbers.

Examples: VII (5 + 1 +1)
XXV (10 + 10 + 5)
CLX (100 + 50 + 10)

For the numbers 4 and 9, and any numbers that begin with them, use **subtraction**.

Examples: 4 is IV (5 − 1)
9 is IX (10 − 1)
90 is XC (100 − 10)

Big Time

For very large numbers, a bar is placed over a number to show that it is multiplied by 1,000. For example, 10,000 is $\overline{X}$ (10 x 1000); 4,000 is $\overline{IV}$ (4 x 1000).

It's a Date!

Can you crack the code of these number problems? First, convert the Roman numerals to Arabic numbers. Then do the arithmetic. When you're done, you'll know the date the safety pin was invented.

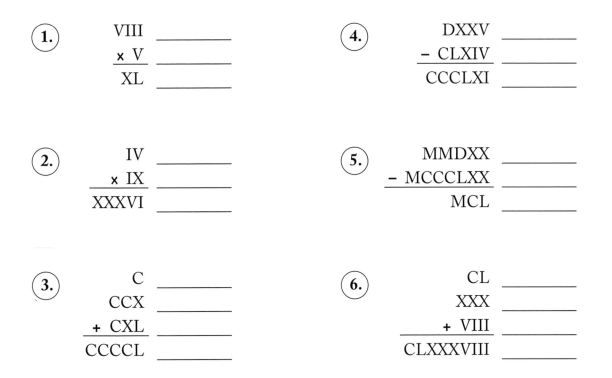

1.
VIII _____
x V   _____
XL   _____

4.
DXXV   _____
– CLXIV   _____
CCCLXI   _____

2.
IV   _____
x IX _____
XXXVI _____

5.
MMDXX   _____
– MCCCLXX   _____
MCL   _____

3.
C   _____
CCX   _____
+ CXL _____
CCCCL _____

6.
CL   _____
XXX   _____
+ VIII   _____
CLXXXVIII _____

Write the answer to each of the problems in the spaces below. Do the arithmetic. Then you'll know when the safety pin was invented. The answer is on page 154.

1. _____ + 2. _____ + 3. _____ + 4. _____ + 5. _____ – 6. _____ = _____

The safety pin was invented in (circle answer):

   1849   1925   1650

Pyramid Power

Take a closer look at the pyramid on the back of the dollar bill. Notice the Roman numerals at the base of the pyramid? What date is on the pyramid?

A Great Pick-Me-Up

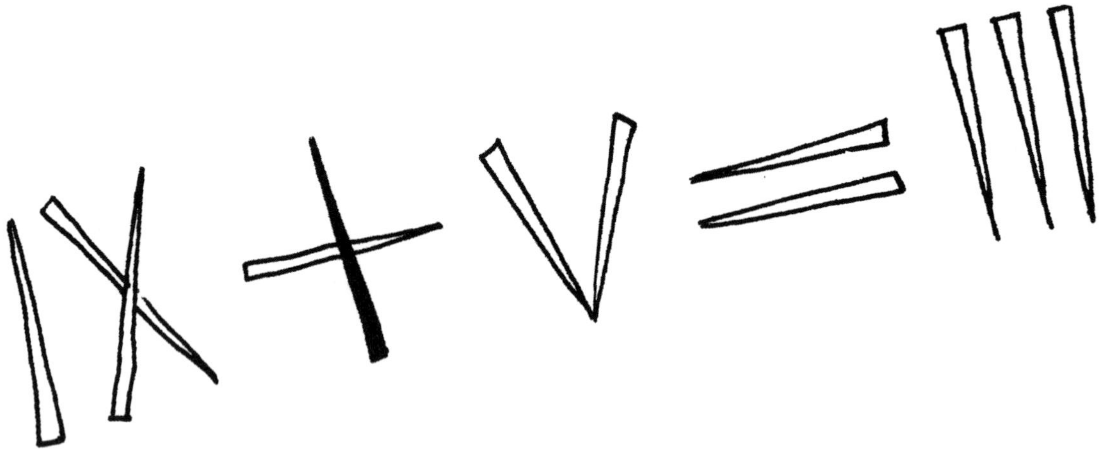

You will need toothpicks for this challenge. Lay out your toothpicks to match the puzzles below. Then take the challenge! (Answers on page 154).

1. **IX + V = III**

Move one toothpick to correct.
(Hint: Look above.)

2. **IV = IV − I**

Move one toothpick to correct.

3. **I = I = II = I**

Move two toothpicks to correct.

4. **XI + I = X**

Getting tired? Well, this one is "self-correcting." You don't have to do anything. Just look at it upside down. Pretty neat, huh?

Finger-Picking Fun

Take 12 toothpicks and lay them down to make 4 squares.

Can you remove just 2 toothpicks to make 2 squares instead of 4?

Take 9 toothpicks and lay them down to make this figure.

Can you remove just 2 toothpicks to get 3 triangles?

Can you remove 3 toothpicks to get 1 triangle?

Can you remove 4 toothpicks to get 2 triangles?

Can you remove 6 toothpicks to get 1 triangle?
(Answers are on page 154).

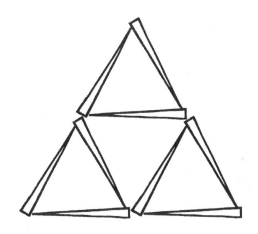

Make up puzzles with a friend. Experiment. Move toothpicks. Add or take away toothpicks.

The Pick of the Pack

An equilateral triangle is a triangle that has three equal sides.

You can make an equilateral triangle with three toothpicks, like this:

It is possible to make four triangles by using just six toothpicks.

Can you do it? (You will need to break some toothpicks to make them shorter and you may need to use some tape to keep them together.) Answer is on page 155.

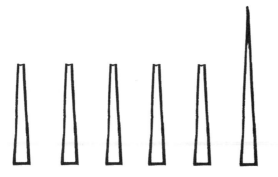

Top Secret!

A good way to keep secrets safe is to write them in code. Here's a code that is based on a special grid. The numbered lines go across. The symbols go up and down. There are letters where the two lines meet. For example, the letter R is at point 4+. So 4+ is the code for R. Is your name Rachel? Then send a note and sign it 4+. Only your friend will know who the note came from.

	*	•	+	~	#
1	A	B	C	D	E
2	F	G	H	I	J
3	K	L	M	N	O
4	P	Q	R	S	T
5	U	V	W	X	Y
6	Z				

Here's a riddle for you.

What starts with an E, ends with an E, and has one letter in it?

Here is the answer in code. It is an: 1#   3~   5•   1#   3•   3#   4*   1#.

Break the code. Put the answer here: E __ __ __ __ __ __ __.

Do you want another riddle?

What did Paul Revere say at the end of his ride?

He said: 5+   2+   3#   1*

__ __ __ __

Answers on page 155.

Write your own riddles and share them with friends. Or use this space to send a secret message.

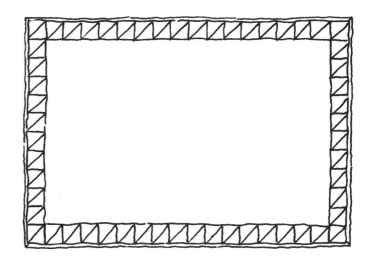

Boxed In

This code is simple—once you know the secret. Use the code box to get the number that stands for each letter. For example, the number for R is 34 (3 for the column that R is in and 4 for the row that R is in).

This is how to put your message in code. First, write the message. Then find the code numbers for each letter. For example:

H	E	L	P
32	51	23	14

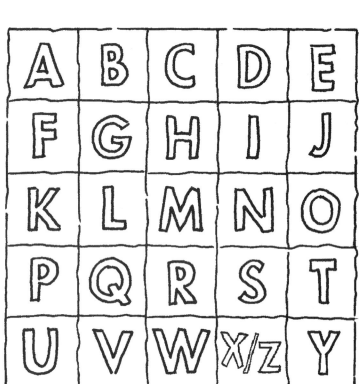

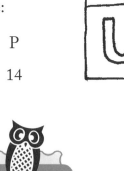

Fun Fact

Loose Lips Sink Ships

Navy code books are locked in the captain's safe, but if a ship is in trouble, the captain must throw the code books overboard. The code books are covered in heavy lead. This way, they'll sink to the bottom of the ocean fast, and no one will be able to break the navy's code!

Fun Fact

Old Ways Are Best?

The ancient Greeks sent long-distance messages. But they wrote them on their servants' heads! They'd shave a servant's head and write a message. The servant would wait for his hair to grow in. Then he'd set out to deliver the message. When the servant reached his destination, his head would be shaved. The other person would read the message. How's that for using your head?

It's All Greek!

People used to say something was "all Greek" when they couldn't read or understand it. Do the letters on this page look Greek to you? Well, they are! You can use the letters of the Greek alphabet to make a secret code. You'll notice that some letters are missing! Just use our alphabet for the missing letters.

Α Ψ Δ Φ Γ Ξ Κ Λ   Π Θ Ρ Σ Τ Θ Ω 6 Χ Υ Ζ
A B C D E F G H I J K L M N O P Q R S T U V W X Y Z

Laugh Track

If you can "uncode" these riddles, you'll have the last laugh. Answers are on page 155.

Why is the number nine always full?

— —
Β Ε Ψ Α Θ Σ Ε   Ι Τ   Ψ Ο Μ Ε Σ   Α Φ Τ Ε Ρ   Ε Ι Γ Η Τ

Which is the luckiest of numbers?

— —
Τ Η Ε   Ν Θ Μ Β Ε Ρ   Ο Ν Ε   Β Ε Ψ Α Θ Σ Ε   Ι Τ   Α Λ 6 Α Υ Σ   6 Ι Ν Σ

Hidden Numbers

The sentences on this page are tricky. Each one contains a hidden number spelled out with consecutive letters. Can you find all of them? Answers are on page 155.

Example: Pat <u>won</u> the race.

(The hidden number is two.)

1. At camp we have fun in every kind of weather.

2. We watched both reels of film in total silence.

3. We only need half our lunch time to eat.

4. We try to watch our favorite shows even when we're tired.

5. There are books on every shelf in the library.

6. Steffi vents her anger by singing loudly.

7. Can you guess the height of that monument?

8. I enjoy it when my cousins visit often.

9. I can make a sand tunnel even if it's too cold to go swimming.

10. Pat went your way home yesterday.

1. _____   6. _____

2. _____   7. _____

3. _____   8. _____

4. _____   9. _____

5. _____   10. _____

What Are You Worth?

Are you worth more than Tom Cruise? More than Jennifer Lopez? Are you worth more than a Big Mac? You can find out right now.

In this money box, each letter is worth some money. **A** is worth 1¢, **B** is worth 2¢, and so on.

A 1¢	B 2¢	C 3¢	D 4¢	E 5¢	F 6¢	G 7¢
H 8¢	I 9¢	J 10¢	K 11¢	L 12¢	M 13¢	N 14¢
O 15¢	P 16¢	Q 17¢	R 18¢	S 19¢	T 20¢	U 21¢
V 22¢	W 23¢	X 24¢	Y 25¢	Z 26¢		

Write your name on a piece of paper. Take each letter one at a time and write down what each letter is worth. Add up the numbers of your first and your last name. The total is how much your name is worth.

How do you compare?

Suppose your name is Jennifer.

J = 10
E = 5
N = 14
N = 14
I = 9
F = 6
E = 5
R = 18
81¢

Need Some Advice?

There are five proverbs hidden in this puzzle. To find one, pick a number from one to five. Look for the boxes with the number you've picked. Then write the letters in order from left to right. When you're done, figure out the sayings by separating the letters into words.

2 TW	4 AB	1 AS	3 DO	4 IR	5 AP	1 TI	5 EN	3 NT
5 NY	3 CO	2 OH	4 DI	3 UN	5 SA	2 EA	3 TY	4 NT
1 TC	4 HE	3 OU	5 VE	1 HI	4 HA	5 DI	3 RC	5 SA
4 ND	2 DS	3 HI	4 IS		3 CK	2 AR	5 PE	3 EN
3 SB	5 NN	4 WO	5 YE	1 NT	4 RT	3 EF	5 AR	4 HT
2 EB	1 IM	4 WO	2 ET	3 OR	5 NE	2 TE	1 ES	4 IN
2 RT	4 TH	3 ET	1 AV	2 HA	4 EB	3 HE	5 D	1 ES
1 NI	3 YH	4 US	2 NO	3 AT	4 H	1 NE	2 NE	3 CH

Can you figure out the sayings that are pictured on this page? Answers are on page 155.

Square Deal

There's a secret message hidden on this page. Solve the problem in each box. Circle the words in the boxes that equal 100. Put the words in order to get the message.

72 + 40 IT	10 x 11 BOAT	63 + 37 ARE	47 + 50 MAY	85 + 65 WOW
36 + 65 WHERE	20 x 5 A	17 + 84 MATH	9 x 11 SMART	50 ÷ 10 WISE
39 + 62 BUY	82 + 33 SECRET	49 + 51 KID	102 − 4 AND	76 + 26 CHART
71 + 19 FIRST	112 − 16 LUCK	84 + 6 MAY	28 + 71 BRING	100 ÷ 10 SNOW
82 + 18 YOU	10 + 10 TRY	15 + 19 WHERE	41 + 58 KEEP	4 x 25 GREAT

MESSAGE: _____

Answer is on page 155.

It's a Fortune!

No one can predict the future. You can have fun trying!

1. Cut a piece of paper so you have a perfect square. Fold it once on the diagonal. Then unfold it.

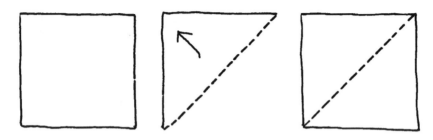

2. Fold the paper on the other diagonal. Then unfold it.

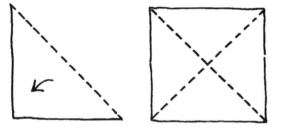

3. Fold in each corner to the middle point. Run your fingernail over the folds to be sure they stay. Write the name of a color on each corner flap.

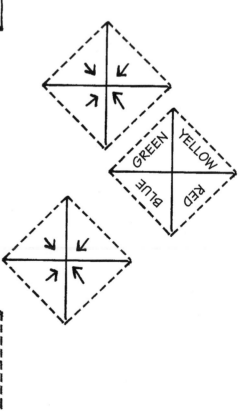

4. Turn the folded paper over. Again, fold each of the four corners into the middle and press.

5. Now you have eight triangles. Number them.

6. Open the triangles. Write a fortune under each number.

   (Example: You will get a surprise phone call.)

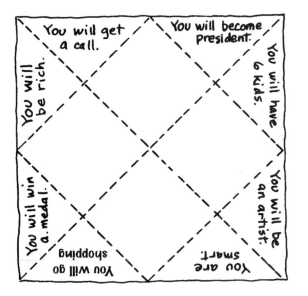

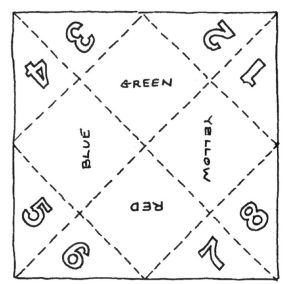

7. Fold the fortune flaps back in. Now fold the square in half to make a rectangle.

8. Place your thumb and fore fingers under the color flaps on each side of the rectangle. Push the outside edges toward the center so that the four color flaps come together in a point. Practice opening and closing the fortune-teller by moving your fingers side-to-side, together and apart.

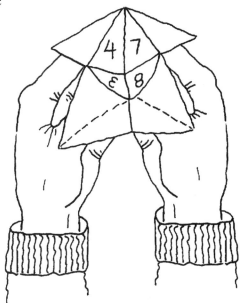

To play, ask a friend to choose a color. Open and close the fortune-teller for each letter of the color. Leave the fortune-teller open and have your friend choose a number from those visible inside the fortune-teller. Open and close the fortune-teller that number of times. Then have your friend pick another number. Again, open and close the fortune-teller. Then leave it open and have your friend choose a third number. This time, lift up that corner and read the fortune.

Test of Champions (duh!)

Are you suffering from brain drain? Then this test is for you. It's guaranteed to make you feel like a champ!

1. Which shape does not belong?

2. What number belongs in this series?

   1   2   3   ?   5   6   7

3. How many inches are in a 12-inch ruler?

4. Without lifting your pencil from the paper, connect the dots.   •   •

5. How many circles are in this picture?

6. Can you help the mouse find the cheese?

7. Which animal is taller?

8. Write your age _____.

   Add 5. Subtract 5. The answer will be your age!

9. If you have three cheeseburgers, how many do you have?

10. Which is the greatest amount?

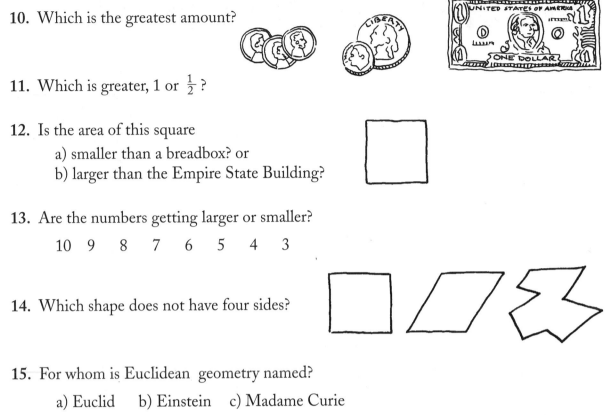

11. Which is greater, 1 or $\frac{1}{2}$?

12. Is the area of this square
    a) smaller than a breadbox? or
    b) larger than the Empire State Building?

13. Are the numbers getting larger or smaller?

    10   9   8   7   6   5   4   3

14. Which shape does not have four sides?

15. For whom is Euclidean geometry named?

    a) Euclid   b) Einstein   c) Madame Curie

16. Which is a symbol for money?

17. What time is it when the big hand is on 12 and the little hand is on 3?

18. Six kings in England have been named George, the last one being George the Sixth. Name the previous five.

19. Spell *parallelogram.*

20. Explain trigonometry or write your name in CAPITAL LETTERS.

21. What was Albert Einstein's first name?

22. How long did the Thirty Years' War last?

BONUS QUESTION (worth three points)

23. Why isn't your nose 12 inches long? (Answer on page 155.)

Numbers with an "Attitude"

You use numbers to add and subtract every day. For example: 5 + 9 = 14. But what about 5 − 9? Is it possible to get an answer? Sure. Your answer will be a negative number.

Negative numbers describe quantities that are less than zero. Think of the coldest day imaginable. In some places, the temperature drops below zero and there might be temperatures of −10° or −15°, for example.

The number line below will help you visualize positive and negative numbers. If you start at zero and go right, you get positive numbers. If you move to the left, you get negative numbers.

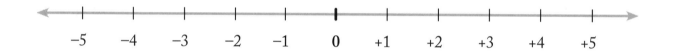

$$-5 \quad -4 \quad -3 \quad -2 \quad -1 \quad 0 \quad +1 \quad +2 \quad +3 \quad +4 \quad +5$$

Which Way?

Use the number line to help you calculate the following:

A. 3 + (− 5) = _____

B. 5 + (− 3) = _____

C. (−3) + (−2) = _____

D. (−4) + (−2) = _____

Answers are on page 155.

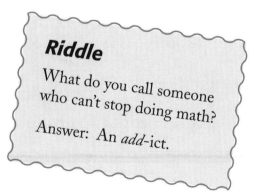

Riddle

What do you call someone who can't stop doing math?

Answer: An *add*-ict.

In Good Shape:
Geometry and Patterns

How good are your powers of observation?
You'll need a keen eye to "see" the many shapes
around you and find examples of symmetry.
You'll also have a chance to "draw" on what you
know and "noodle out" some fun doodles.

Shape Up

Take two squares and cut each one on the diagonal. Now you have four triangles to work with. How many shapes can you make?

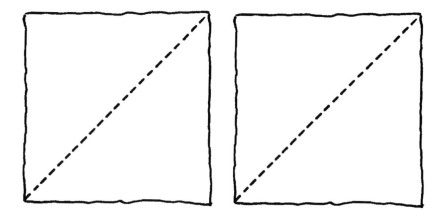

Note: You can trace these squares onto another piece of paper and cut them out to use. Draw the shapes you make on this page.

1. How many triangles, or three-sided shapes, can you make?

2. How many quadrilaterals, or four-sided shapes, can you make?

3. How many pentagons, or five-sided shapes, can you make?

4. How many hexagons, or six-sided shapes, can you make?

Not So Square, After All

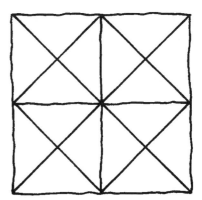

Did you ever think you could have so much fun with a square?

Square Deal

How many different squares can you find?
Can you find 10?

Connect the Dots

Connect the dots to make designs. How many designs can you make?

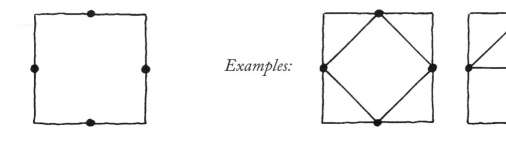

Examples:

Shades of Fun

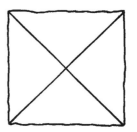

This square is divided into four small triangles. How
many ways can you shade two triangles? What about one
triangle? Three? Four? Can you come up with 15 ways to
shade the small triangles? Answers on page 155.

Right on the Dot

Can you draw a
square with one of
these dots on each
of its four sides that
does not touch any
of these words?

Count on It

Look at the picture of the kite.

How many triangles can you count? 10? 20?
25? More?! Can you come close to 50?

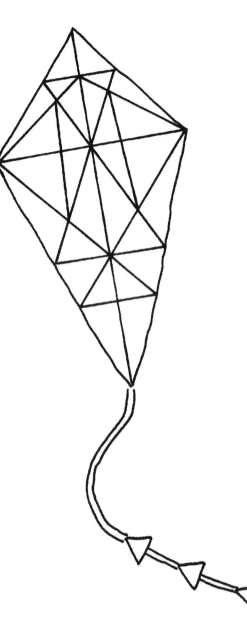

Be a Star!

How many triangles can you count in this star?
Can you come close to 60?

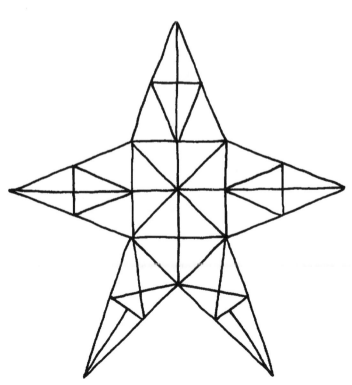

Triangles

How many triangles can you find in your home? Outside your home? What kinds of triangles can you find?

ISOSCELES

EQUILATERAL

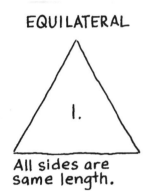

1.

All sides are same length.

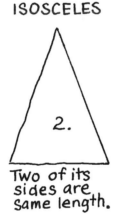

2.

Two of its sides are same length.

RIGHT ANGLE

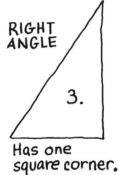

3.

Has one square corner.

Copy this triangle on a piece of paper. Then cut it apart to get nine small triangles. Rearrange the triangles to make different shapes. Can you make a parallelogram? Can you make a square? Can you make a rectangle? Can you make a hexagon?

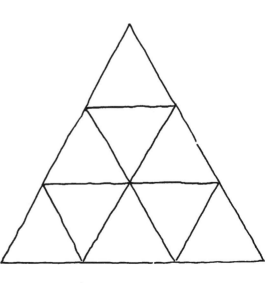

What Do You See?

Try another way of looking at lines and shapes. Can you figure out the "doodles" on this page? Answers are on page 155.

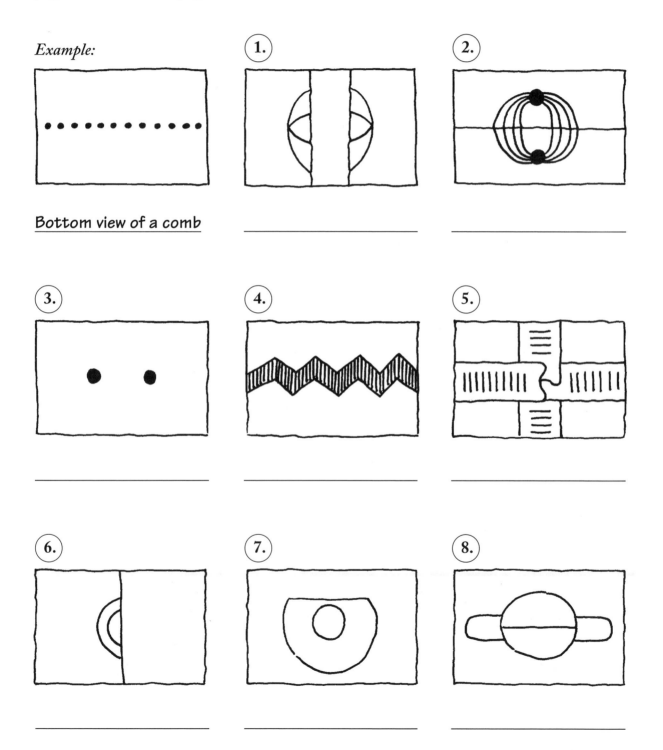

Example:

Bottom view of a comb

1.

2.

3.

4.

5.

6.

7.

8.

Hole in One!

You will need:

> a pencil
> a dime
> a quarter
> a piece of paper
> scissors

Directions:

- Put the dime on the paper.

- Draw a circle around it.

- Cut along the circle to make a dime-sized hole.

Now tell your friends that you can push a quarter through the hole without tearing the paper.

How is that possible?

Fold the paper so that the fold passes across the hole. Now take the ends of the fold and bend them toward each other. You will see the circumference of the hole has now been flattened out or stretched. This way, the quarter will slip easily through the hole.

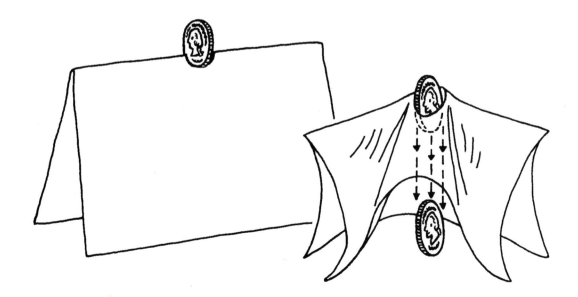

Camp Knotty Pine

There are five cabins in the girls' section of Camp Knotty Pine. The cabins are all connected by paths. How many paths are there? Answers are on page 155.

Pyramid Power

Before they roast marshmallows at Camp Knotty Pine, they use them to build things. Get your own marshmallows and toothpicks and join them.

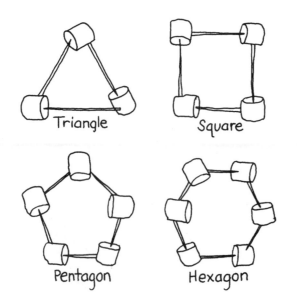

Boys' Night Out

The boys at Camp Knotty Pine went hiking and then went to sleep under the stars. When you figure out which camper is in which sleeping bag, write his name on it. Here are the clues:

- Scott and Jim like the same girl but don't especially like each other. They went to sleep as far away from each other as possible.

- Sam is next to Pete but not next to Daryl.

- Daryl is sharing music with Jim, who is nearest the food chest.

- Sam is friends with Scott but isn't sleeping next to him.

- Rick is next to Sam but not next to Scott.

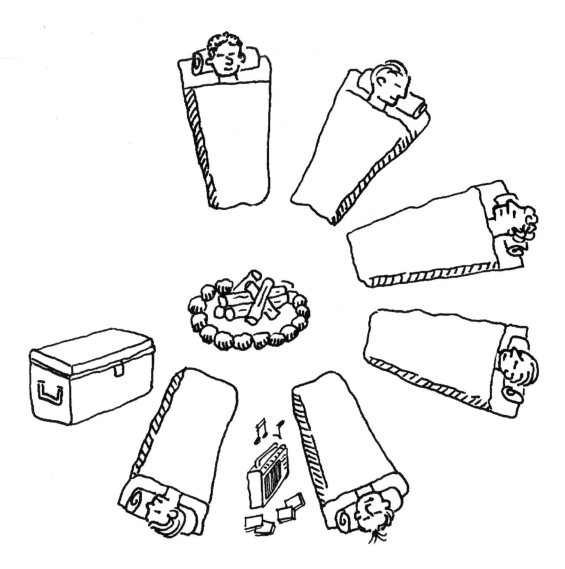

Heart to Heart Symmetry

Imagine folding a heart shape in half. One half would look exactly like the other. In art and nature, things are often balanced or *symmetrical*. A line that divides a figure into two halves that are mirror images of each other is a *line of symmetry*.

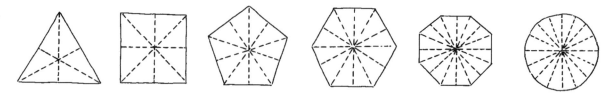

The next time you go outdoors, look for things that have symmetry (leaves, for example). Tour your own home. What examples of symmetry can you find? Look at your body in the mirror. Is it symmetrical?

Cut out three or four different shapes with symmetry. Put them together to make one large symmetrical shape.

Does a parallelogram have symmetry?

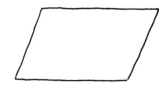

What numbers, when written, have symmetry?

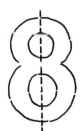

Symmetry makes for beautiful designs. Be creative. Come up with an original design for a new wallpaper, pillow cover, or gift wrap. Experiment with colors and patterns.

Face It

The human body has symmetry. There are two arms and two legs, one on each side. But the human face is not symmetrical. Each side is slightly different. The left side expresses more unpleasant feelings than the right side. Yet, this is our "secret" side. When you look at a person, the right side of the person's face is the part your brain recognizes or "sees."

Here's an odd fact. The face you see in the mirror is not the same face others see. When you look at your own face in the mirror, you are seeing a mirror image.

Would you like a peek at the secret sides of people? Find a photograph of a friend or relative taken straight on. Place an unframed mirror at a 90° angle along the center of the face. Look along the angle formed by the mirror and photo to see how the face would look if it were made of two right or two left sides.

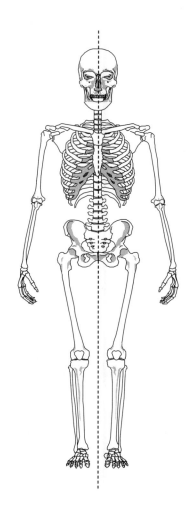

Fun Fact

The Eyes Have It

Did you know that the pupils of your eyes enlarge, or dilate, when you look at someone you love? Your pupils shrink, or contract, when you look at people you don't like.

The Shape of Things to Come

How many funny critters will "shape up" on this page? Copy each illustration step-by-step to make crazy critters. Then use combinations of shapes to make up your own.

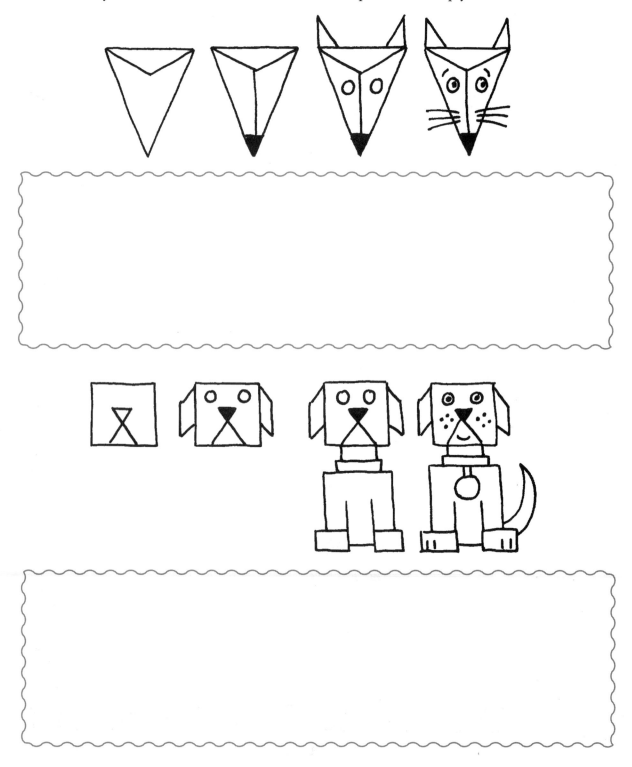

Hands-on Math

Things to Make and Do

Here's your chance to use what you know to
create math masterpieces—everything from party
decorations to wall hangings to crazy cutups.
You'll design original quilt patterns, create
tangram pictures, and draw geometric critters for
fun. So have your scissors and glue ready. You'll
need them now.

Fair and Square

Many things you make from paper require that you start with a square. Here's a neat way to make a square from a rectangular piece of paper.

Fold side AC to line up with side CD.

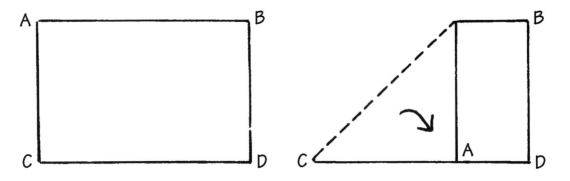

Cut off single layer of paper as shown.

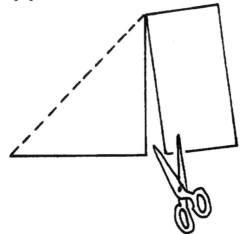

Unfold the paper to get a perfect square.

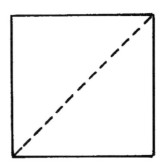

The Last Straw

What good is having a straw if you don't have a cup to drink from? Not to worry. You can make a cup. Here's how. All you need is a piece of waxed paper. It should be about 10 inches square.

1. Fold the square to make a triangle.

2. Find the midpoint of each edge and mark it.

3. Fold the left-hand corner to the middle of the opposite edge.

4. Fold the right-hand corner to the midpoint of the other edge.

5. Now you have two small triangles on top. Fold one down toward you. Then turn the cup over. Fold down the other small triangle.

6. Open your cup. Get out your straw. Get ready to drink up!

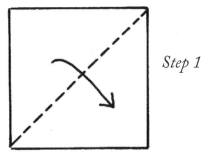
Step 1

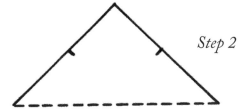
Step 2

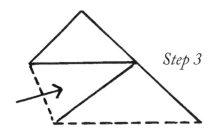
Step 3

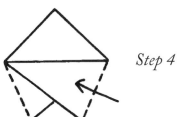
Step 4

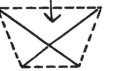
Step 5

Hint

Keep a "folded cup" with you in your backpack. Then you can wet your whistle whenever you feel like it.

Step 6

Class Act

You will need:
  sheet of construction paper
  pencil
  scissors

Directions:

1. Cut the paper in half to get two pieces, approximately 4" × 11".

2. Pleat one piece of paper back and forth.

3. Draw the outline of half a person against the folded edge. Be sure the figure goes all the way across to the other edge.

4. Cut the figure through all the layers and unfold.

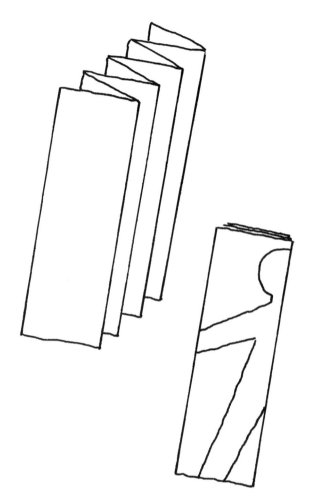

Partner Pals

Try making two figures with your second piece of paper.

1. Make your pleats a little wider.

2. Draw an outline of half a figure against the folded edge. Draw an outline of half of another figure against the other edge. Be sure their hands join.

3. Cut out and unfold.

You can make your circle of friends out of bright gift-wrap paper. Use it as a party invitation, wall decoration, party hat, or to dress up a present or birthday cake.

Designing Quilts from Square One

You can make a paper quilt for hanging or you can make a fabric quilt. All you need are different colored or patterned squares.

Square Off

There are 6 ways to cut squares to make patchwork patterns and designs.

For 2 large triangles, do this:

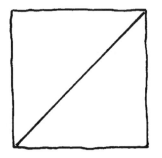

For 2 large rectangles, do this:

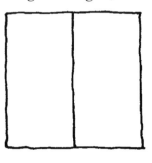

For 4 medium triangles, do this:

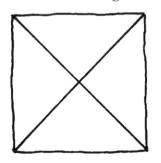

For 4 strips, do this:

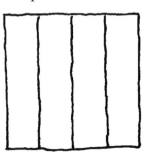

For 8 small triangles, do this:

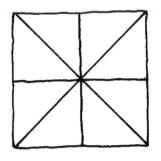

For 4 medium squares, do this:

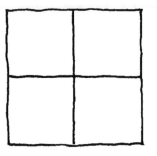

Piece by Piece

Once you've cut some squares, you can put the pieces together in interesting ways. Experiment. Here are some designs you can make by placing triangles, squares, and strips of different fabrics or colors next to each other.

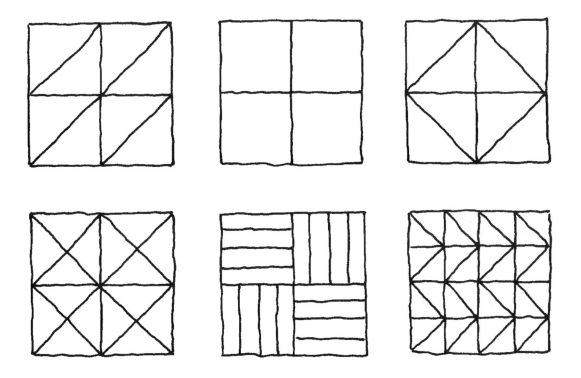

And "Sew On" . . .

If you are working on a paper quilt, glue your pieces together. If you are working with fabric, sew your pieces together. Then sew squares together to get bigger and bigger square blocks. Real quilters sew their patchwork tops to quilt batting (fluffy material) to get a padded fabric result.

Tangram Art

Do you notice the seven shapes in the square? Each shape is called a "tan." You can create original tangram designs by putting the pieces together in different ways to form different pictures.

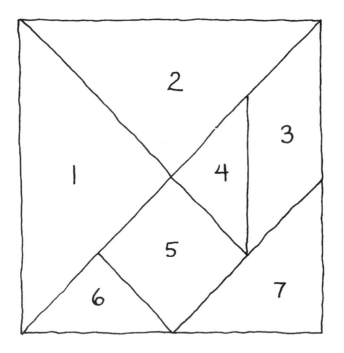

Trace the seven tans onto stiff paper and cut them out. Try copying some of the designs you see below. Make up your own tangram pictures.

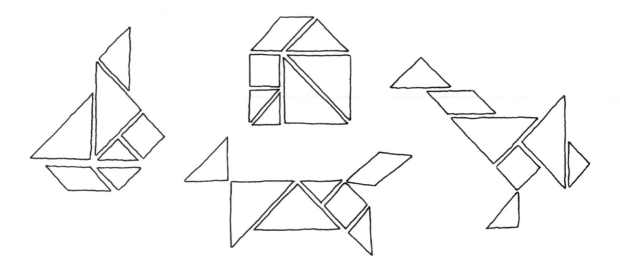

Reach for the Stars

Follow the directions to make a hanging star. You can hang one or more stars from your ceiling, or you can make stars for party or holiday decorations.

You will need:

>   scissors
>   glue
>   construction paper

Directions:

1. Cut 12 strips of construction paper, 2" x $8\frac{1}{2}$" each.

2. Fold a paper strip in half, then open it.

3. Fold each half in half again so the ends meet at the center fold.

4. Overlap the two ends and glue them together to make a triangle.

5. Repeat to make all 12 triangles.

6. Glue 6 triangles together (points facing in) to make a hexagon.

7. Glue the remaining 6 triangles to the sides of the hexagon (points outward).

8. Make two holes in the top triangle and use thread or yarn to hang the star.

Star Power!

Use different-colored construction paper to create interesting patterns.

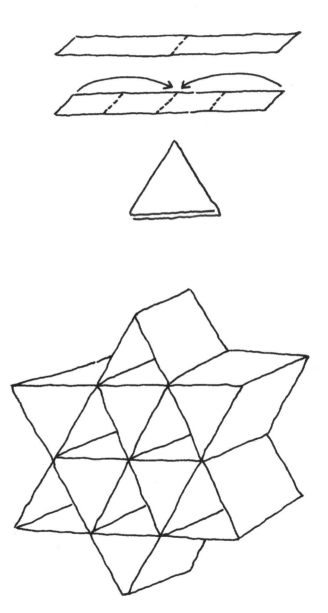

Circle with a Twist

What You Need:

    paper

    ruler

    scissors

    tape

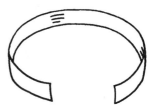

What to Do:

- Cut out a piece of paper. Make it about 1" wide and 11" or 12" long.

- Make a circle by bringing the ends of the paper together.

- Now twist the paper and tape the ends together.

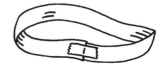

Now you have a circle with a twist—a kind of "magic circle." Why is it magic? To find out, cut it down the middle the long way. What do you think will happen? Will you get two circles? Or . . . will you get a *magic circle?*

The Möbius Strip

You've just created a Möbius strip, named after mathematician August Möbius, who invented it in 1858.
Möbius was known for his work in the branch of mathematics known as *topology* (the study of spatial relationships of geometrical structures). Why is the Möbius strip special? Well, think of it this way. Every piece of paper is supposed to have two sides. So, for example, you could color one side red and the other side blue. But a Möbius strip has only one side and one edge.

Time and Money:

Tidbits, Rib Ticklers, and Coin Tricks

You spend it. You save it. Some of you even earn it. But that's not all you can do with money. In this section, you'll read some far-out facts, learn some neat coin tricks, and play games of strategy—all involving money. But, first, there's a brief "time-out" in which you can pick up some timely tidbits about time itself.

Money Talks

It's About Time

What time is it when the clock strikes 2400? Time to get the clock fixed? No, it's time to start a new day. In the military, people don't divide the day in A.M. and P.M. hours. Instead, they use a 24-hour clock. The hours are numbered from 1 to 24.

The A.M. hours are easy to figure out. They go from 0000 (midnight) to 1200 (noon). For example, 8:00 A.M. would be 0800. (That's "0–8 hundred hours.")

The P.M. hours go from 1201 (1 minute after noon) to 2400 or 0000 (midnight). That means that 6:00 P.M. would be 1800, 18–hundred hours. Here's a tip: To change P.M. hours into 24-hour time, write the time using 4 digits and then add 12 to the hours. For example, 3:00 P.M. in military time is found as follows: 0300 + 12 = 1500 hours.

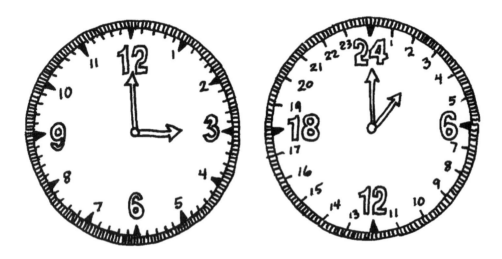

Give the standard time and military time for each.

What time do you wake up?   _____ _____

What time do you start school?   _____ _____

What time is school over?   _____ _____

When do you go to bed?   _____ _____

What's your favorite time of day?   _____ _____

A Real Clock Stopper

Tell a friend to choose any number on a clock and *not* tell you what the number is. It will be up to you to get the number.

Here's how:

Explain that while you tap the clock face with a pencil, your friend should count each tap silently, starting with the number after the one he or she chooses. For example, if the number is 8, your friend should start counting silently with 9. If the number is 6, the count should start with 7. Instead of the count of 20, your friend should say "Stop!"

To make the trick work, you must count silently, too. Tap any numbers you like for the first *seven* taps. On the eighth tap, touch 12. After that, tap backward (11, 10, 9, and so on) until your friend says, "Stop." Your pencil will be on the correct number.

The Time of Your Life

Having the "time of your life" means having a great time. What do you like to do to have the time of your life?

> **Riddle:** What animal keeps the best time?
>
> **Answer:** A watchdog.

Time Teasers

Why couldn't they keep a clock in jail?
Because time is always running out.

Why did the girl sit on her watch?
She wanted to be on time.

Why shouldn't you tell secrets in front
of a clock?
Because time will tell.

What time is it when 10 dogs chase
a cat down the street?
Ten after one.

What are always moving, but never
going anywhere?
The hands of a clock.

Fun Fact

Catching Some Zs

Did you know that you
spend about one-third
of your life sleeping?
That's equal to 2,920
hours a year. How many
hours have you dozed
so far? Multiply your age
by 2,920. Tired, anyone?

Can you guess the time expressions
pictured here? How many others do
you know? Answers are on page 155.

1.

2.

3.

4.

Fun Fact

Ancient Times

The ancient Egyptians didn't have clocks. They probably used the moving shadow of the sun to tell time on sundials. But sundials only work in daylight. How did the ancient Egyptians tell time at night? They used a water clock. This "clock" was a water-filled pot that had a small hole in the bottom. Markings on the side of the pot represented the passage of time. As time passed, the water level moved down. People probably "read" the time by noting the water level.

Time Out

If you "saved time," what would you use your extra time to do? What do you wish you had more time for? Think of the good times you've had. What was the best of times?

Fun Fact

Sun's Up!

The sunflower got its name because it is *heliotropic*. That is, it always faces the sun. Have you ever heard of a flower-bed clock? It's possible to grow a garden that tells time. For example, morning glories open up in the morning. Certain other flowers open at 7:00, others at 8:00, others at 9:00, others at 10:00, others at noon. Then there are the evening primroses. The night-blooming cereus opens at about 10:30 or 11:00 at night.

It's Only Money

Crazy Eights!

Imagine you empty your pockets and find the following coins:

Using eight coins at a time, can you come up with each total below? Name the coins that make up each total. Answers are on page 155.

A. 34¢   **B.** 44¢   **C.** 63¢   **D.** 78¢

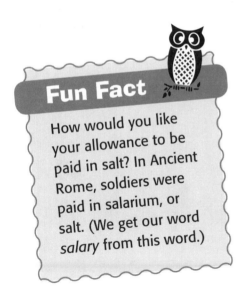

Fun Fact

How would you like your allowance to be paid in salt? In Ancient Rome, soldiers were paid in salarium, or salt. (We get our word *salary* from this word.)

The Dancing Dime

You can make a dime "dance" without touching it. Here's how. Put a dime on the top of an empty soft-drink bottle. Wet your finger and run it around the bottle rim to seal the opening. Hold the bottle in both hands for about 15 seconds (one-Mississippi, two-Mississippi, and so on). The dime will slowly move up and down.

What's happening? The heat from your hands makes the air inside the bottle expand. The warm air pushes up the dime. Now remove your hands. The dime will keep "dancing" until the bottle cools.

Presidential Race

Here's a chance for Thomas Jefferson and Abraham Lincoln to square off face-to-face. It's a game for two players. But you'll need 4 nickels and 4 pennies to play. Put the coins on the grid as shown or make your own game board. (Divide a square of paper into 16 parts, 4 rows of 4 squares each.)

How to Play:
Each player chooses a president (either Jefferson or Lincoln). Players take turns moving their coins in any direction, one square at a time. (Jumping coins is not allowed.)

Object of Game:
The winner is the player who gets all four of her or his coins in a row, beyond the first row, either across, down, or diagonally.

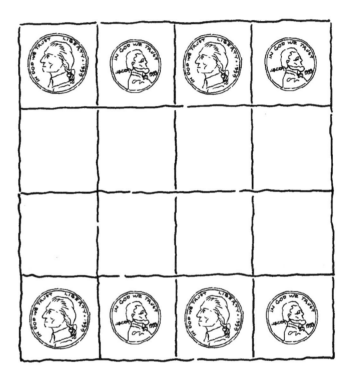

Coining Phrases

How many of these money expressions do you know?

break the bank	small change	
cold cash	pocket money	money talks
a dime a dozen	easy money	make money
the buck stops here	mad money	a penny for your thoughts

Switch!

Can you get the dimes and nickels below to change places?

Place your own coins on the empty top row as shown in the bottom row. Here's how to make the switch: You can slide a coin into an empty space next to it. Or you can jump a coin sideways, as long as you land on an empty space.

How many moves does it take you?

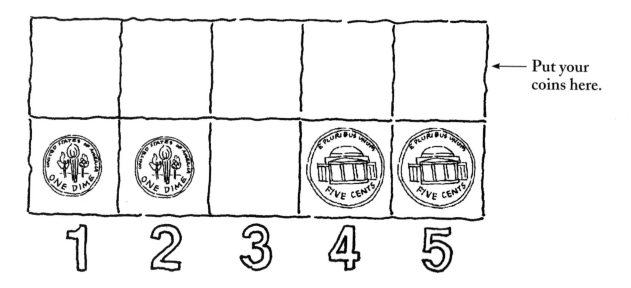

← Put your coins here.

Need Some Help?

Fill in the spaces below to make the switch in only eight moves.

1. Slide the dime from box 2 to box _____.

2. Jump that dime with the nickel from box 4 to box _____.

3. Slide the nickel from box 5 to box _____.

4. Jump that nickel with the dime from box 3 to box _____.

5. Take the dime from box 1 and jump it to box _____.

6. Slide the nickel from box 2 to box _____.

7. Take the nickel from box 4 and jump it to box _____.

8. Slide the dime from box 3 to box _____.

Coin Trick

Arrange 6 coins as shown. Tell your friend to move only 1 coin to create a horizontal row and a vertical column that each contain exactly 4 coins. Answer is on page 155.

Dollars and Sense

Penny Power

Take 10 pennies and arrange them in a triangle like this. Now, move exactly 3 pennies to make the triangle point down instead of up. Go for it! If you get stumped, the solution is on page 155.

Fun Fact

Passing the Buck

Did you know that paper money has no paper in it? Bills are printed on material made of linen and cotton because it lasts longer. While we're on the subject, ever wonder why we call a dollar bill a *buck*? Before paper money was printed, Americans traded in buckskins. So that's how the slang term *buck* came to be. Do you know other slang words for dollars?

Easy Money

Nickel for Your Thoughts?

Give a friend a penny and a nickel. Have your friend put one in each hand, without showing you which is where. Give your friend a multiplication problem for each hand. For example, say, "Multiply what's in your right hand by 16." When your friend is done, say, "Now multiply what's in your left hand by 14."

Tell your friend to add the two numbers. Then you say which hand the nickel is in.

The Secret:
It's easier to multiply by 1 than by 5. So, it will take your friend longer to multiply by the nickel. You'll know which hand holds the nickel by the time it takes your friend to multiply.

Bank on It!

Would you like to see your money grow? Fill a glass two-thirds full with water. Drop a quarter into the glass. Look down at the glass at a slight angle. Your quarter will appear larger because the curvature of the glass acts as a magnifier. (A smaller image of the quarter appears to float above the first image because light is bent at the surface of the water.)

Fun Fact

Do you carry money in your wallet? If you had lived on Yap Island years ago, you might have had to *roll* it along! People there once used large stones for money. Yap Island is in the Pacific Ocean about 850 miles east of the Philippines.

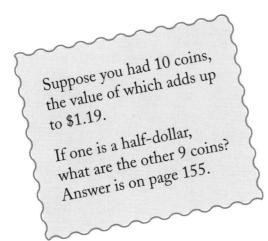

Suppose you had 10 coins, the value of which adds up to $1.19.

If one is a half-dollar, what are the other 9 coins? Answer is on page 155.

Big Bucks

Your friends will be amazed when you tell them that you can guess how much money (not counting coins) they have with them.

Give your friend the following directions:

- Look at all the paper currency you have. Write down the sum of the values of all the bills.

- Now double that number.

- Add 1 to the above number.

- Multiply that number by 5.

- Now add 5 to the result.

- Next, multiply the result by 10.

- Subtract 100 from the above number.

Now ask your friend to tell you the number. Divide the number by 100 and you will get the amount of money your friend has.

Suppose your friend has a $5 bill and two $1 bills.

$$5 + 1 + 1 = 7.$$
$$7 + 7 = 14$$
$$14 + 1 = 15$$
$$15 \times 5 = 75$$
$$75 + 5 = 80$$
$$80 \times 10 = 800$$
$$800 - 100 = 700$$
$$700 \div 100 = 7 \,!$$

Do the Math

Suppose your friend has $12.

Double it.   _____

Add 1.   _____

Multiply by 5.   _____

Add 5.   _____

Multiply by 10.   _____

Subtract 100.   _____

Divide by 100.   _____

Did you end up with $12?

Heads or Tails?

Here's a trick your friends will "flip" over. You'll be able to tell whether a coin hidden under someone's hand is head or tail side up.

Choose someone from the group and give the person these directions:

1. Tell the person to put a handful of coins on a desk or tabletop—say five or six. Tell the person to spread out the coins so everyone can see them and so that they're not too close together.

2. Now turn your back and tell the person to turn over as many coins as she or he wants. But each time your friend turns a coin, she or he must call out "FLIP."

3. Next, keeping your back turned, tell the person to choose any coin and cover it with his or her hand or fingers.

4. Now turn around. You'll be able to say whether the coin under your friend's hand is heads or tails. (But pretend to think for a moment!)

How the Trick Works:

1. When the coins are arranged on the table, secretly count how many are heads-up.

2. Each time the person says, "Flip," add one to this number, counting silently to yourself until the person is done. Remember this total.

3. If your total is an even number, there will be an even number of heads-up coins on the table. So when you turn around, count the heads-up coins you see. If you see an odd number of heads-up coins, it means that the coin under your friend's hand must be heads—to make the total equal. But if you see an even number of heads on the table, the hidden coin must be tails.

4. What if your secret total is an odd number? It means that there will be an odd number of heads-up coins on the table. So if you turn and see an even number when you look, you'll know that the hidden coin is heads. If you see an odd number of heads-up coins on the table, the hidden coin must be tails.

Making Change

Here's your final challenge. Can you switch the nickel with the dime in less than 20 moves? You can move one box at a time, but not diagonally. Solution is on page 155.

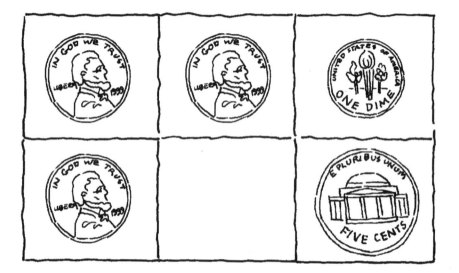

Heads Up!

Did you know that U.S. law forbids showing living persons on money? If a new coin were minted, whose picture would you put on it? Why?

Calculator Math:
Enter Laughing

Did you know how you could do tricks with your calculator? You can make fancy figures, create words, and even double-check your addition. In this section are cool calculator riddles, tricks, and ways to use your calculator to amuse yourself and surprise your friends.

Arithmetricks

Use your calculator to do these problems. Write down each answer. Then turn your calculator upside down to get the answer to the question. Answers are on page 155.

A. A spider has eight of these: _____

$$3295 + 2342 = \text{_____}$$

B. When a lobster is surprised, it's called _____ shock.

$$93528 - 16183 = \text{_____}$$

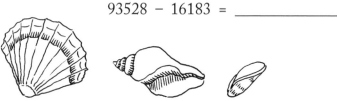

C. The famous book: *For Whom the* _____ *Tolls.*

$$3122 + 4616 = \text{_____}$$

D. The opposite of *more*: _____

$$9463 - 3926 = \text{_____}$$

Make up your own calculator messages by translating the following numbers into letters:

0 → O	1 → I	2 → Z	3 → E	4 → H
5 → S	6 → G	7 → L	8 → B	9 → G

Write your words backward (because you turn the calculator upside down). If a word ends in 0, push the decimal point after you enter 0.

C-o-o-l Calculations

One for All and All for One

Here's a "one-derful" multiplication trick. Use a scientific or graphing calculator for speed. Watch a neat pattern emerge. Answers are on page 156.

11	111	1111	11111
x 11	x 111	x 1111	x 11111

111111	1111111	11111111	111111111
x 111111	x 1111111	x 11111111	x 111111111

Going, Going, Gone (Well, Almost)

Do these problems with your calculator. Now what happens?

9 × 12345678 + 9 = _____

9 × 1234567 + 8 = _____

9 × 123456   + 7 = _____

9 × 12345   + 6 = _____

9 × 1234   + 5 = _____

9 × 123   + 4 = _____

9 × 12   + 3 = _____

9 × 1   + 2 = _____

From Start to . . . Start!

For more calculator fun, try this a few times. What do you discover?

- Start with a three-digit number that doesn't repeat any digits.
- Multiply that number by 2.
- Add 4.
- Multiply by 5.
- Add 12.
- Multiply by 10.
- Subtract 320.
- Cross out the zeros at the end.

Suppose you pick the number 754.

754
754 × 2 = 1508
1508 + 4 = 1512
1512 × 5 = 7560
7560 + 12 = 7575
7575 × 10 = 75,720
75,720 − 320 = 75,400
75,400
754

Fancy Figure Eights

Do you want to see something cool? Look at this.

$$0 \times 9 + 8 = 8$$
$$9 \times 9 + 7 = 88$$
$$98 \times 9 + 6 = 888$$
$$987 \times 9 + 5 = 8888$$
$$9876 \times 9 + 4 = 88888$$
$$98765 \times 9 + 3 = 888888$$
$$987654 \times 9 + 2 = 8888888$$
$$9876543 \times 9 + 1 = 88888888$$

Stack Them

Use your calculator to continue the following.

$$1 \times 8 + 1 = 9$$
$$12 \times 8 + 2 = 98$$
$$123 \times 8 + 3 = 987$$
$$1234 \times 8 + 4 = \underline{}$$
$$12345 \times 8 + 5 = \underline{}$$
$$123456 \times 8 + 6 = \underline{}$$
$$1234567 \times 8 + 7 = \underline{}$$
$$12345678 \times 8 + 8 = \underline{}$$
$$123456789 \times 8 + 9 = \underline{}$$

Very Calculating

Here's a neat trick to help you double-check large sums of numbers. You can use it to check your addition (whether you use a calculator or not).

First, add the five-digit numbers in the left-hand column. Now add the digits of this answer and note it below. Then go back to the five-digit numbers and add the digits across in each row. Keep adding until you have a single digit. Then add these single digits in the column on the right. If the results agree, you're addition was correct.

Example:

45395	4 + 5 + 3 + 9 + 5 = 26	→ 2 + 6 =	8
20173	2 + 0 + 1 + 7 + 3 = 13	→ 1 + 3 =	4
36942	3 + 6 + 9 + 4 + 2 = 24	→ 2 + 4 =	6
+ 29226	2 + 9 + 2 + 2 + 6 = 21	→ 2 + 1 =	3
131736			21

1 + 3 + 1 + 7 + 3 + 6 = 21

(Note that all of the numbers in your math problem have to have the same number of digits. Above, all of the numbers have five digits.)

Use the same trick for subtraction—except subtract the smaller number from the larger when you have your single digits.

Example:

64592	6 + 4 + 5 + 9 + 2 = 26	→ 2 + 6 =	8
− 33691	3 + 3 + 6 + 9 + 1 = 22	→ 2 + 2 =	(−) 4
30901			4

3 + 9 + 1 = 13   →   1 + 3 = 4

Seeing Double

You won't need glasses, but you'll be "seeing double" when you do the following.

Directions:

- Write any three-digit number.

- Now make a six-digit number by writing the three-digit number twice.

- Divide this number by 7.

- Divide this number by 11.

- Finally, divide the number by 13.

What happens?

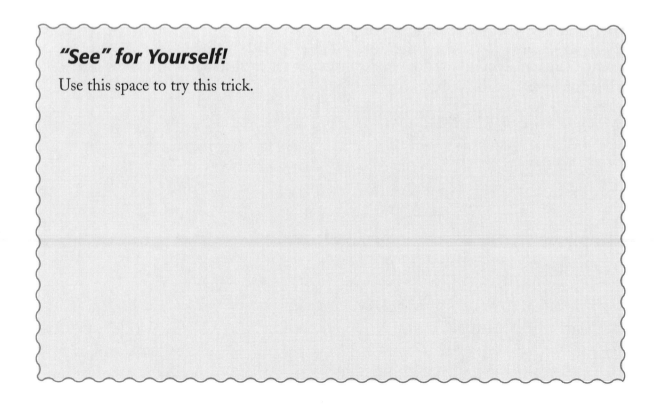

Suppose you write the number 653.

653

653,653

653,653 ÷ 7 = 93,379

93,379 ÷ 11 = 8,489

8,489 ÷ 13 = 653

"See" for Yourself!
Use this space to try this trick.

And the Answer is . . . 73 (always)!

Write 73 on a piece of paper and fold it up. Give this paper to your friend before you start.

Directions to tell your friend:

- Select a four-digit number.

- Enter it twice into a calculator.

- Divide the number by 137.

- Now divide this number by your original number.

Tell your friend to unfold your paper. Your friend will be shocked that you had the correct answer all along.

No matter how many times you try this trick, the answer will always be 73!

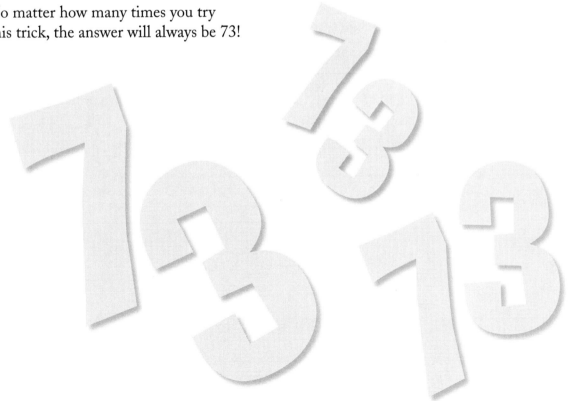

Suppose your friend picks the number 4561.

4561

45614561

45614561 ÷ 137 = 332953

332953 ÷ 4561 = 73

That Crazy 8 Trick

Here's another calculator trick that will stun your audience.

Directions:

- Have someone pick a number between 1 and 9.

- Have the person use a calculator to multiply that number by 9, and then by 12,345,679.

- Have the person show you the result— you'll be able to tell him or her the original number right away!

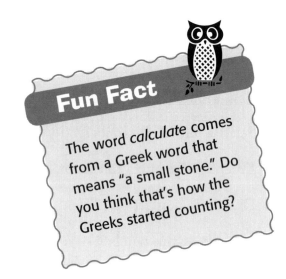

Fun Fact

The word *calculate* comes from a Greek word that means "a small stone." Do you think that's how the Greeks started counting?

The Secret:

This trick is really quite simple.

If a person selects 5, the final answer is 555,555,555.

If the person selects 3, the final answer is 333,333,333.

How can this be? The reason is: 9 × 12345679 = 111111111.
So whatever number a person selects, it is multiplied by 11111111.

Why is the trick called a "Crazy 8 Trick"?

The eight-digit number (12,345,679) you use is easily memorized because only the 8 is missing from the sequence!

Four-Step Magic

For this trick, all you'll need is one friend and one calculator.

1: Have your friend think of a number from 1 through 100 and write it down without showing you the paper.

2: Now, using your calculator, take your age, multiply it by 2, add 5, multiply by 50, and subtract 365.

3: Next, keep that number from your last step on the calculator and hand the calculator to your friend.

4: Tell your friend to add his or her "secret number" to the number already on the calculator, then add 115 to it.

Voila!

The first half of the resulting number is your age, and the other part of the number is your friend's secret number!

Step Up to the Plate

1. Say your friend writes down the number 35.

What you do:

2. 12 (your age) x 2 = 24

24 + 5 = 29

29 x 50 = 1450

1450 – 365 = 1085

3. Give the calculator to your friend with 1085 still displayed.

What your friend does:

4. 1085 + 35 = 1120

1120 + 115 = 1235

Your age is 12, and the secret number is 35!

Boomerang Math

No matter what you do, you'll always get the number you started with. See for yourself.

Try this:

- Write down any number.

- Multiply the number by 3.

- Add 2.

- Now multiply by 3 again.

- Add a number that is 2 more than the number you started with.

- Drop the final digit.

You're back to the number you started with!

Suppose you pick the number 450.

450

450 x 3 = 1350

1350 + 2 = 1352

1352 x 3 = 4056

4056 + 452 = 4508

450

Use Your Head

Choose a one- or two-digit number and use your head to work on the trick.

Calculator Time

Choose a three- or four-digit number and use your calculator to practice the trick.

The Great Divide

Here's another "boomerang" trick.

You'll need your calculator. Then follow the directions, look at the example, and spring it on a friend!

Directions:

- Choose a three-digit number.

- Repeat the number to create a six-digit number.

- Multiply this six-digit number by 9.

- Divide by 11.

- Divide by 7.

- Divide by 3.

- Multiply this answer by 2.

- Divide by 13.

- Divide by 6.

Suppose you pick the number 452.

452

452,452

452,452 x 9 = 4,072,068

4,072,068 ÷ 11 = 370,188

370,188 ÷ 7 = 52,884

52,884 ÷ 3 = 17,628

17,628 x 2 = 35,256

35,256 ÷ 13 = 2,712

2,712 ÷ 6 = 452

Hint:

Read the directions aloud as your friend does the calculations.

Right Back at You

Here's a cool number trick that will add up to fun.

Tell a friend to:

- Enter a three-digit number on a calculator.
- Add 242.
- Subtract 38.
- Add 96.

Have your friend tell you the answer. You can guess your friend's starting number by subtracting 300 from the answer.

> Suppose your friend enters the number 214.
>
> 214
>
> 214 + 242 = 456
>
> 456 − 38 = 418
>
> 418 + 96 = 514
>
> Your friend tells you the answer so far is 514.
>
> 514 − 300 = 214

Let the Games Begin:

Paper, Pencils, and Partners

You'll sharpen your wits and skills with the games in this section. Do a cross number puzzle, work with a logic box, reason through mind benders, or graph your favorite jokes. There are many Ideas for games to do alone—like when you're on a long car trip. But there are also games to play with partners. What do all these games have in common? Some skill, some strategy, and some luck! Whichever you choose, have fun!

Keep It Down!

Here's your chance to play a game in which the low score wins. Move your pencil along the lines from START to FINISH. The object is to choose a numbered route that adds up to the lowest total points. See if you can get your total points below 40. Play alone or with a friend. But remember: Keep it down!

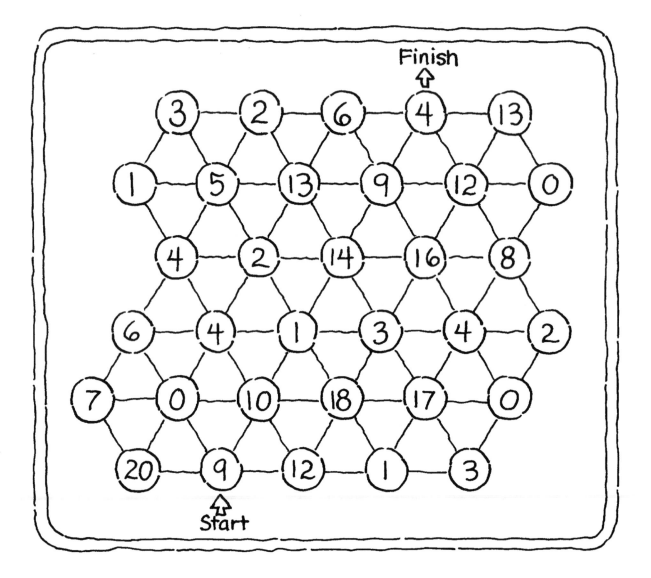

"Sum Feat"

Here's a game you can play by yourself or with a friend or two. Just write the numbers 1 through 9 on a sheet of paper. Do this three times, scattering the numbers around the page (see below).

Choose any number greater than 10. The examples shown are 13 and 32. Move your pencil from number to number until you reach the total. Try to make as many totals as you can. If you are competing with a friend, the one who makes the most "strings of numbers" wins. Remember, you can use any number greater than 10 for your target total.

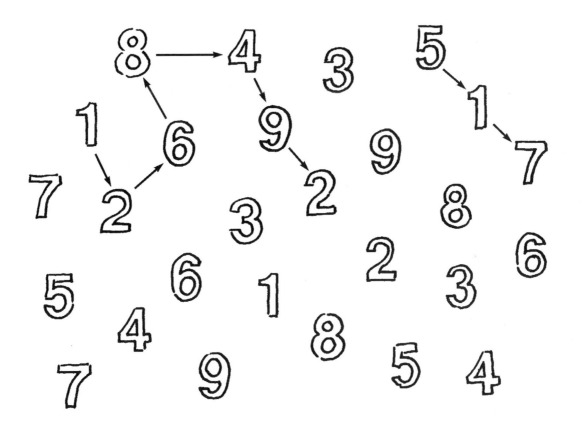

Cross Number Puzzle

This "cross number" puzzle works like a crossword puzzle, except there are numbers, not words, in the boxes. Complete the puzzle. Then make up your own cross number puzzles to challenge your friends. Solution is on page 156.

ACROSS

1. There are _____ inches in a foot.

3. 5 × 5

5. 749 – 516

7. 32 + 52

8. There are _____ minutes in an hour.

9. 144 ÷ 9

11. 88 ÷ 2

13. 352 + 259

15. 775 – 453

17. 12 × 12

19. 51 + 32

20. A "baker's dozen"

DOWN

1. 45 ÷ 3

2. 189 ÷ 3

4. There are _____ U.S. states.

5. There are _____ hours in a day.

6. There are _____ inches in a yard.

7. 6 × 6 + 50

9. 519 ÷ 3

10. 7 x 3

12. 366 + 128

13. 542 + 81

14. 555 ÷ 5

16. 7 × 4

18. 172 ÷ 4

Get the Point?

Notice the point on the grid? You can find it by having your fingers meet at point G6. Starting at the dot, follow the code below to locate other points on the grid. Mark each point with a dot. Then draw one continuous line to connect the dots. See what turns up in the space.

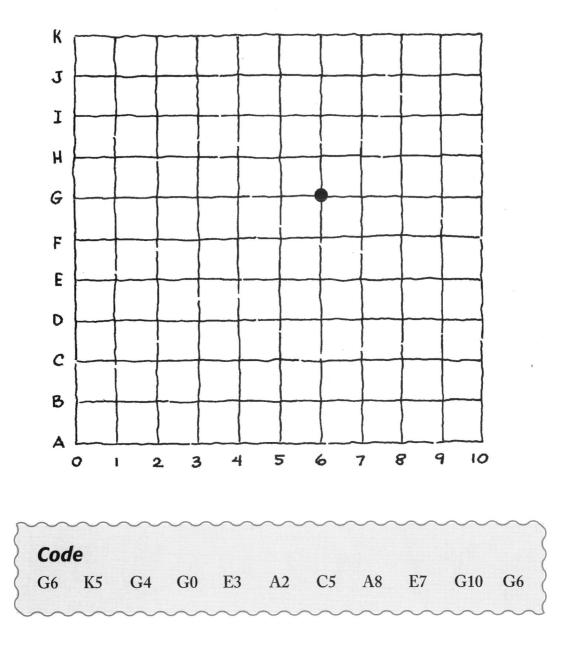

Code

G6   K5   G4   G0   E3   A2   C5   A8   E7   G10   G6

Laugh Track

Ta da! Here's your chance to rate jokes. Read the five riddles and rate each one—from 0 to 10—on the laugh grid. Have a few friends rate the jokes as well. Then compare your responses. Which riddle gets top billing?

Match each riddle with its answer to get a good laugh. (Answers are upside-down at the bottom of the page and also on page 156.) What's your overall reaction to the jokes? To get the average score, divide the sum of the scores by 5.

A. What stories do little puppies like?

B. Why was one puppy jealous of the other?

C. What do you call it when your dog is angry at you?

D. Why shouldn't you fight with a dog?

E. What do you get when you cross a rooster and poodle?

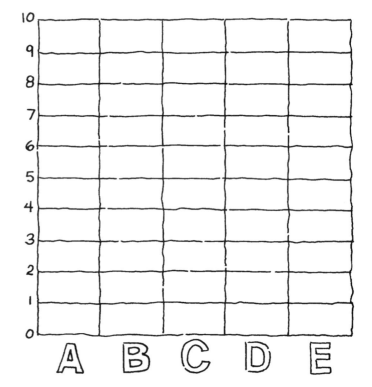

To the Rescue

Two rescue rangers have two animals on Square One Island. They need to get them to Square Two Island. From there, they will take a ferry to the mainland to see a vet. The rangers have a small rowboat. It only takes two animals or people at a time, so they will have to make more than one trip.

The animals may be dangerous. So there should never be two animals together with one ranger on either island. The animals don't get along with each other. So they should never be alone together. How can all four get from Square One to Square Two?

If you can't do this brain teaser in your head, fill in the spaces below. Doing so will help you think through this logic problem.

- On the first trip, one ranger and one animal got to Square Two. Then the ranger returns to Square One. This leaves one _____ on Square Two. Now there are two _____ and one _____ on Square One.

- For the next trip, a ranger and animal cannot go together. That would put two _____ and one _____ on Square Two. So on the second trip, two _____ go to Square Two. Now there are two _____ and one _____ on Square Two. One _____ is alone on Square One.

- Now the boat must go back to Square One. So one _____ rows back to Square One. That leaves a _____ and an _____ on Square Two.

- For the last trip, the _____ and the _____ row from Square One to Square Two. That puts everyone on Square Two.

Ancient African Game

You can use an egg carton to play the game *Wari* or *Mancala* with a friend.

You will need:

an egg carton
48 small stones

How to play:

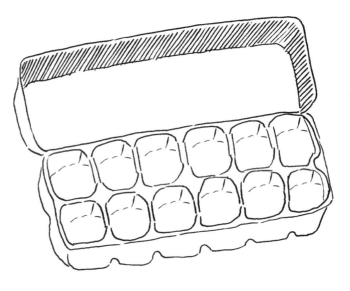

1. Sit at a table with the egg carton between you so that each player's side has six compartments.

2. Each player gets 24 stones and puts four in each of the six compartments on his or her side of the carton.

3. Take turns. First, take out all game pieces from one of your compartments. Then drop them one by one into the next four compartments, moving counterclockwise around "the board." If you reach the end of your side of the board, move up to the first compartment on your opponent's side and continue moving counterclockwise through his or her compartments.

4. If the last piece you drop falls on your opponent's side *and* the total number of pieces in that compartment is either two or three, you get to "capture" those pieces. Take out the captured pieces and hold them on the side.

5. Your opponent then takes his or her turn, picking up all pieces in one of his or her compartments and dropping them around the board, as you did.

6. The game continues until all of one player's compartments are empty and it is that player's turn. The player who has the most captured pieces is the winner.

Eggs-ceptional Aim

You will need:

   egg carton

   large black marker

   pennies or beans

Directions:

Mark each of the 12 spots on the egg carton with a number value. Each player gets five tries to land three pennies in the spaces by tossing pennies from a distance. Add up each player's score to get the winner. The highest score wins. You can vary the game by making one space a "free throw" space. You can also vary the game by having the lowest score win.

It's a Wrap!

Here's a logic mystery for you to "unwrap." Jayna bought presents for her three friends—Jennifer, Jason and Jud. She sent someone to deliver the presents, but she forgot to put name tags on them. See if you can figure out who gets what. Read the clues and use the chart to match the people with their presents.

Clues

1. Jenn's present is wrapped in polka dot paper.

2. The polka dot present is soft and squishy.

3. The present with smiley faces is not for Jason.

4. The present in striped paper is long and narrow.

The Chart

When you are sure which person gets a certain gift, put a check in the person's box in the chart on the next page. Put an X in a person's box when you know he or she does not get a certain gift.

Getting Started . . .

Clue Number 1: *Jenn's gift is wrapped in polka dot paper.*

The box is already marked with a check to show this. The box is also marked with Xs to show that Jason and Jud's gifts are not wrapped in polka dot paper. Place Xs to show that Jenn's gift is not wrapped in striped paper or smiley face paper.

Clue Number 2: *The polka dot paper is soft and squishy.*

The only present that's soft and squishy is the one in the polka dot paper. So Jenn is getting that gift. You can check Jenn's box next to the teddy bear. You can put Xs in the boxes for the other gifts under Jenn. Because you know Jenn is getting the teddy bear, you can put Xs in the other people's boxes next to that gift.

Clue Number 3: *The gift with smiley faces is not for Jason.*

You can put an X in that row under Jason's name. That means that Jason's present must be wrapped in the _____ paper. Check Jason's box for that paper. Put an X in Jud's box for that paper.

There is one name and one kind of paper left. That means that _____'s gift is wrapped in _____ paper. Check Jud's box next to that paper.

Clue Number 4: *The present wrapped in striped paper is long and narrow.*

The only present that is long and narrow is the _____. Because _____ has the striped paper, he must be getting that gift. Check his box next to that gift. Mark an X under his name for any other gift.

Because Jason is getting the watch, you know that _____ isn't. Put an X in Jud's box for that gift. That means that Jud must be getting the _____. Check that gift in Jud's box.

Wrap It Up!

Look at your chart and complete the mystery. The solution is on page 156.

Jenn is getting the _____ wrapped in _____ paper.

Jason is getting the _____ wrapped in _____ paper.

Jud is getting the _____ wrapped in _____ paper.

	Jenn	Jason	Jud
polka dot paper	✔	✘	✘
striped paper			
smiley face paper			
wrist-watch			
CD			
teddy bear			

Battle of Wits

This game for two players dates back to Ancient Egypt and is known also as "Nine-Men Morris." To play, use the game board on the facing page. Each player will need nine markers, such as checkers, coins, or buttons. The object is to capture seven of the other player's markers.

How to play:

1. Decide who will go first. Players take turns putting markers on the board. Only one marker may be put on a spot.

2. Players try to get three markers in a row that are connected by line segments. A row may be vertical or horizontal, but not diagonal. The players also try to keep their opponents from getting a row of markers.

3. Each time a player gets three markers in a row, he or she removes any one of the other player's markers that isn't in a row of three.

4. When all the markers are on the board, players take turns moving their markers. Markers must be moved along a line segment to the next spot.

5. Each player tries to get three markers in a row while blocking the other player from doing it.

6. Each time a player gets a row of three markers, he or she captures a marker that isn't in a row of three.

7. When a player has three markers left on the board, he or she may move a marker anywhere on the board.

8. A player wins when the other has only two markers left on the board.

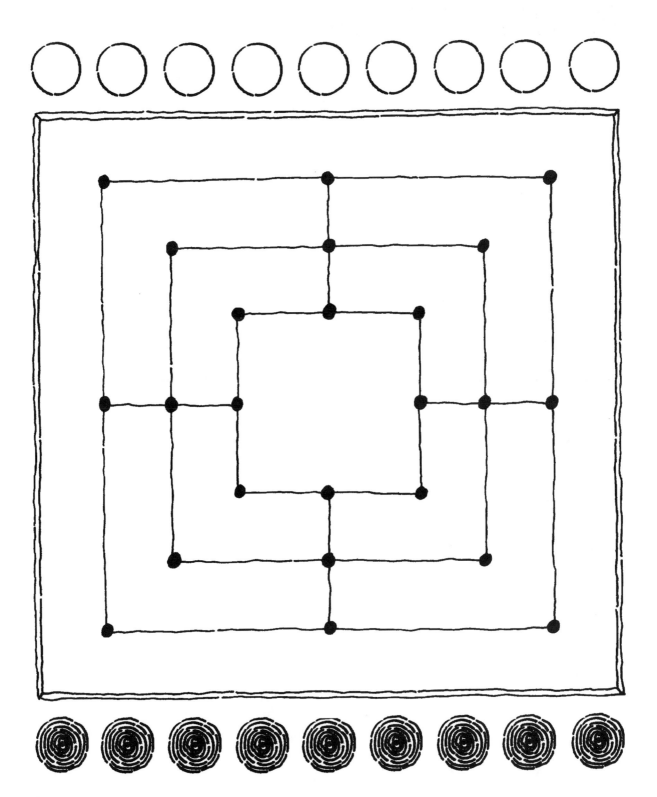

Fractured Speech

What would happen if you started writing in fractions?

For example, you might write the words "I understand" this way: $\dfrac{\text{stand}}{\text{I}}$

Here are a few fractured sayings. Under each one, write what you think it means. Then make up your own. See page

$$\dfrac{\text{fell}}{\text{board}} \qquad\qquad \dfrac{\text{they}}{\text{ate}} \qquad\qquad \dfrac{\text{wearing}}{\text{coat}}$$

_____ _____ _____

Ready for a greater challenge? See if you can read each sentence below. The answers are on page 156.

1. $\dfrac{\text{stand}}{\text{I}}$ how hard this task is.

2. But before $\dfrac{\text{took}}{\text{you}}$ the challenge, I knew you'd do well.

3. I will $\dfrac{\text{be}}{\text{joyed}}$ when you get all the answers right.

4. I $\dfrac{\text{have}}{\text{heard}}$ that this is no easy feat.

Fun with Fractions

- I am a unit of time. I am $\frac{1}{7}$ of a week. What am I?

- I am a fraction. My denominator is 14. I am not just a part of one whole thing. I am one whole thing! What fraction am I?

- I am a fraction. My numerator is an odd single digit. My denominator is a single digit that is four times as great as my numerator. What fraction am I?

The Finish Line:

Celebrate with a Mathathon!

This may be the last chapter, but it's not really the end of the book. You'll be flipping around and revisiting pages time and time again. In this section, you'll find ideas for hosting a "mathathon sleepover" and a Math Olympics party. So celebrate in style and pick up ideas for making pop-up invitations, food displays with eye appeal, math costumes, and games and "brainers" you can count on for "googols" of fun.

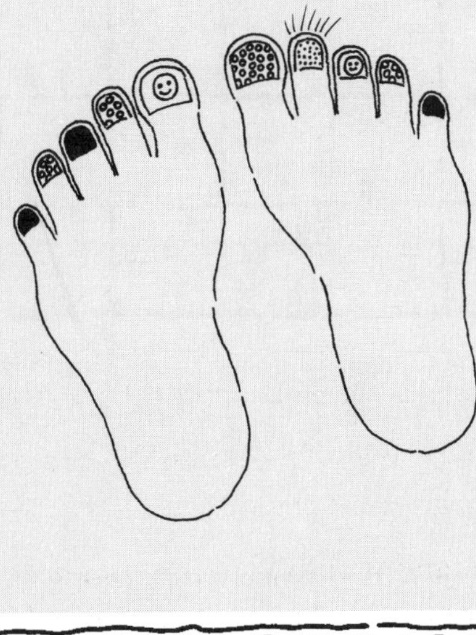

Party!

Rejoice! School's cool, but now it's time to party. Suppose five of your friends are meeting you at the party. See if you can figure out who arrived first, second, and so on. The answer is on page 156. Here are the clues:

1. The five friends showed up at 5-minute intervals.

2. Bethany was the first to arrive.

3. Keesha arrived 10 minutes after Samantha.

4. Bethany and Ivan were dancing when Paul arrived.

5. Paul arrived 5 minutes after Keesha.

6. Samantha ate all the chips before Ivan got there with the dip.

	1	2	3	4	5
Bethany					
Keesha					
Ivan					
Paul					
Samantha					

Recipes for Party Success

Sandwich Triangles

Use dark and light breads for making sandwiches. Trim off the crust. Then cut each sandwich into four mini-triangles. Arrange the sandwiches in symmetrical patterns.

Veggies

Have a lot of raw vegetables on hand, such as carrots and celery. Arrange these in symmetrical patterns on platters. See if someone at home has a recipe for making a sour cream or yogurt dip.

Dessert Shapes

Work with an adult to choose and follow a recipe for making "circle cookies." For contrast, bake "brownie or datenut squares." Remember: You will be using math each time you follow a recipe.

Costumes

As the host you might dress as a Count or Countess. Have your guests also dress in outfits that have to do with numbers. For example, two "crazy eights" ideas would include an *octopus* (eight tentacles) and a *stop sign* (octagon shape). Provide a list of number prefixes to stimulate ideas.

1	uni–	unicycle and unicorn
2	bi–	bicycle and binoculars
3	tri–	triangle and triplets
4	quad–	quadruped (an animal with four legs)
5	pent–, penta–	pentagon
6	hex–, hexa–	hexagon
7	hepta–	heptathlon (a seven-event competition)
8	oct–, octa–, octo–	octave
9	nona–	nonagon
10	dec–, deca–	decade
100	cent–	centipede

Put Your Best Foot Forward
(and Polish Up on Fractions and Decimals)

Are you planning a sleepover? With a little nail polish and a good sense of humor, you can create a night to remember—and a neat way to review math. The idea is simple. Divide into teams. Work together to paint your nails in crazy ways that can be described in math terms. Then put your best feet forward to challenge the other team.

Example:

- Four of the ten toes shown below have polka dots. You can say four-tenths have polka dots.

- You can write four-tenths as a fraction: $\frac{4}{10}$ or $\frac{2}{5}$.

- You can write four-tenths as a decimal: 0.4.

Are you catching on? What can you say about the other toes? You could say 0.2 have funny decals. You could say that 0.3 have dark polish. You could say 0.1 has light polish with sparkles.

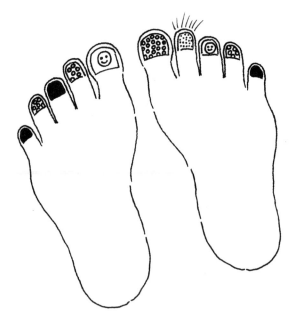

If you have lots of funky nail polish, everyone can go to work. Write a decimal and fraction to describe each set of toes on your team. Make up crazy combinations and challenge the other team to write decimals and fractions for each color and design they see.

You can use the feet on this page for planning. How, for example, does this set of toes strike you?

- 0.3 pale blue

- $\frac{2}{10}$ yellow

- More than $\frac{3}{10}$ with sparkles

- 0.2 lavender or deep purple

- Less than 0.4 with dots

Have fun polishing your nails. But don't forget to "polish off" lots of popcorn as they dry!

Paint me

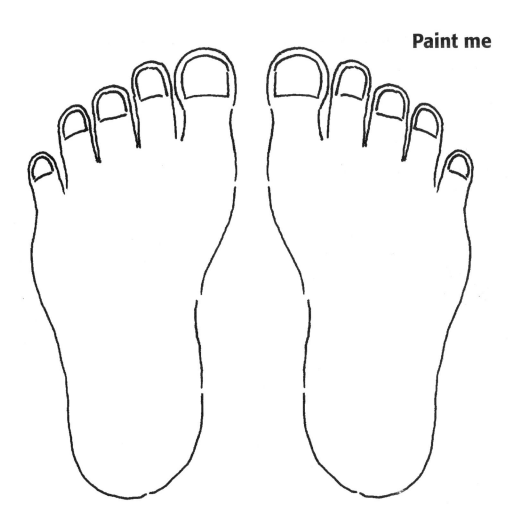

You're Invited!

Would you like to throw a party that's special? Invite your friends to a "mathathon party" and challenge their creativity. Ask a few friends to help you prepare ahead of time. You can follow the directions on these pages for making pop-up invitations. The next few pages will have more ideas for activities. Choose those you think will add up to fun.

Pop-up Invitations

1. Fold a sheet of paper in half. Measure a 2-inch horizontal line from the center of the fold and cut it.

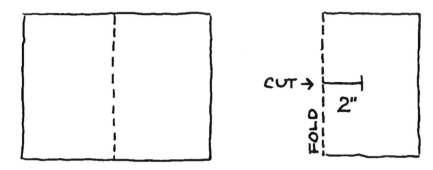

2. Fold two flaps along the cut and crease both folds. Fold them the opposite way and crease again.

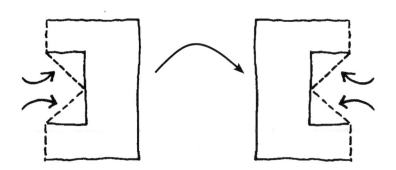

3. Unfold the paper. The creases will make a diamond. Push the top and bottom of the diamond toward you from the back. Crease all the folds. Draw a count or math monster around the "mouth."

4. Put a second sheet of paper behind the first and lightly outline the mouth on it. Then write your "message" inside the outline.

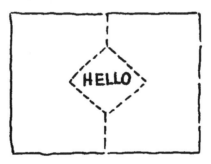

5. Fold the second paper in half, then open it. Paste it to the original card to make an outside cover. You can decorate the cover or write your party details on it.

Math Olympics

Raise team spirits with these Olympic feats of physical and mental might.

You will need:

   a watch with a second hand or a stopwatch
   paper
   pencils
   calculators
   newspaper
   eggs
   oranges
   measuring spoons
   apples and apple peelers
   balls
   yardstick or tape measure

Team 1	48
Team 2	31
Team 3	46

Average 41.6 ≈ 42

Physical Feats

For each feat, get the time of every member on each team. Then find the average score for each team. The team with the highest or lowest average wins, depending on the activity. (To find an average, add up the times of all members and divide the total by the number of people on the team. Round to the next highest whole number.)

Indoors:

• How long can people hold their breaths? Stand on one foot? Stare without blinking? Keep from smiling in spite of funny faces, and so on?

• Have one member from each team take the apple challenge. Tell each person to try to peel the apple in one continuous strip. The person with the longest apple peel wins.

• Hand out sheets of newspaper and copies of directions for making a cup (see page 95). Using the same directions to fold the newspaper will provide party hats for everyone to wear. The first team to make and put on hats wins.

Outdoors:

• How far can kids jump? How far can they throw balls? Experiment with balls and objects of different sizes.

• Place a raw egg in a measuring spoon and have kids move, arms extended, to the finish line without dropping the egg. Experiment. You can use different-sized spoons to vary the challenge.

"Head" Counts

- Challenge individuals from each team with questions you've prepared ahead of time.

  Examples:

  1. Which shape best describes Earth—a cube or a sphere? *(sphere)*

  2. How many planets are in our solar system? *(8*)*

  3. How many ounces in a quart? *(8 oz. in a cup x 4 cups in a quart = 32)*

  4. Add up the following and give the total: Number of players on a baseball team, a football team, and a basketball team. *(9 + 11 + 5 = 25)*

  5. How many feet in a yard? *(3)*   How many inches? *(36)*

  6. Give an expression that has to do with some kind of measurement.
     (Wait a minute; talks a mile a minute; worth its weight in gold, etc.)

- Play a version of *Jeopardy!* by giving answers and having contestants supply math questions. Accept all plausible questions.

  For example:

  Answer: 50 (How many states are in the United States? What is 5 times 10?)

  Answer: 26 (How many letters are in the alphabet? What is 30 minus 4?)

  Answer: 3 (How many congruent sides in an equilateral triangle?)

  Answer: pentagon (What is a 5-sided figure called?)

  Answer: XIV (What is the number 14 in Roman numerals?)

- Provide calculators for players to do problems and "spell" answers.

  Example:

  Press:

7108	What water in a kettle does *(answer: BOIL)*
0.7734	Not goodbye *(answer: HELLO)*
7738	It rings at the end of school *(answer: BELL)*
5318804	What people do in their spare time *(answer: HOBBIES)*
4614	The opposite of low *(answer: HIGH)*

* As of 2006.

Math Workout

Prepare a math bag for each person or team with items they'll need. Staple a scavenger hunt list on the outside of each bag. The first person or team to return from the "math hunt" with a complete and correct list wins. Be sure everyone has the tools he or she needs to do the math work (measuring tape, ruler, etc.).

Bags should contain:

  small box of raisins

  plastic sandwich bag with marshmallows, grapes, and raisins

Room should contain:

  clothing hangers

  at least one coat with round buttons

  food scale, measuring spoons, cups, and so on

  boxes of cereal

Math Challenge

1. Estimate the number of raisins in the small box of raisins (no counting!).

2. Make a mixture of raisins, grapes, and little marshmallows according to the following guidelines: There should be half as many marshmallows as grapes and there should be twice as many grapes as raisins. Put your mixture in the plastic bag and eat the leftovers.

3. Find something in the room that is triangular in shape.

4. List as many circles as you see in the room.

5. About how much does a cup of cereal weigh? How many calories are in a typical portion?

6. How tall is the table? How tall are you? What is the width of the chair? What size waist does the tallest person on the team have?

7. List things that come in cubes.

8. Complete a magic square that has a 5 in its center space. (See pages 26–27.)

9. Name foods that are served up in "fractions."

10. Name five things that come in pairs.

Buzzing Off . . .

A fun way to wrap up the day's activities is with a round or two of Math Buzz. To play, choose a number, such as 5. Then go around the room, counting in turn. Every time a person comes to the number 5 or a multiple of 5, the person whose turn it is must say, "buzz." For example: one, two, three, four, buzz, six, seven, eight, nine, buzz, and so on. The faster you go, and the higher you get, the trickier the game is. For example, the person on whom 55 lands must say, "buzz, buzz."

For an added challenge, do two numbers at once, such as 5 and 7.

You Can Bank on It! (Well, almost)

Here's one last trick you can spring on your folks. But you probably won't be able to hold them to it. Still, they'll be mighty impressed with your math skills.

The next time the issue of allowance comes up, ask for one penny instead of the usual amount. Suggest that each week the amount be doubled. So that means you'll get two cents in two weeks, four cents in three weeks, eight cents in a month.

How long will it take you to reach your present allowance? How long before you're way ahead of it? How long before you imagine going on the greatest shopping spree? How long before your folks cry, "Uncle!" and you're back to your old allowance?

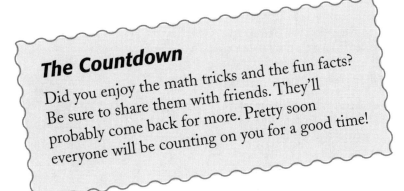

The Countdown

Did you enjoy the math tricks and the fun facts? Be sure to share them with friends. They'll probably come back for more. Pretty soon everyone will be counting on you for a good time!

Answer Key

Answers are provided for many activities. For activities that do not appear here, answers vary.

Birthday Math page 20

Riddle answer: The word *wholesome*

"Sum" Square page 28

Be Creative page 34

2 balls + 2 balls = 1 walk in baseball
2 squares + 2 squares = 1 rectangle
2 colors + 2 colors = 1 color

Seeing Things a "Number" of Ways page 35

Some other possibilities:
threes: feet in a yard, outs in baseball, primary colors, triplets, Musketeers
pairs: man and wife, gloves, hands, feet, shoes, Beauty and the Beast, Ben and Jerry, ham and cheese, Batman and Robin, Wallace and Gromit

And the Number is . . . 395! page 36

1. seven, **2.** sixty, **3.** three, **4.** eight, **5.** thirty-six, **6.** eleven, **7.** seven, **8.** seven, **9.** fifty, **10.** twenty-four, **11.** nine, **12.** fifty-two, **13.** thirteen, **14.** eight, **15.** one hundred

Brain Teasers page 37

Riddle: It had more sense (cents).
1. They both weigh the same—one pound; **2.** Every day does have 23 hours—plus one. Every week does have six days—plus one; **3.** Ten minutes. It doesn't matter how many caterpillars there are; **4.** One is not a nickel. The other is!; **5.** You have the four you took away; **6.** meat; **7.** 35 (50 ÷ 2 = 25 + 10 = 35); **8.** You get 58 every time!; **9.** Two minutes. It takes one minute for the front of the train to get through the tunnel and one more minute for the back of the train to get through; **10.** Six (two red, two yellow, two blue)

The Case of "Finders Keepers" page 38

In every book, odd-numbered pages are always on the right. Therefore, pages 35 and 36 are the front and back of a single page, which means that nothing could have been found between them.

Take Note: Music Adds Up to Fun pages 40–41

1. BAD; **2.** BED; **3.** BEE; **4.** EGG; **5.** AGE

***Sum*sational Wordplay** page 44

1. a square meal; **2.** going around in circles; **3.** six feet underground

Palindromes page 45

57

History: Measure for Measure page 58

Peter Piper . . . a bushel and a peck = $1\frac{1}{4}$ bushels.

Sign On and Be Counted page 62

A. 7; **B.** 5; **C.** 3; **D.** 6; **E.** 8

It's ~~Greek~~ Roman to Me pages 64–65

1. 8 x 5 = 40; **2.** 4 x 9 = 36; **3.** 100 + 210 + 140 = 450; **4.** 525 − 164 = 361; **5.** 2520 − 1370 = 1150; **6.** 150 + 30 + 8 = 188
Safety pin was invented in:
40 + 36 + 450 + 361 + 1150 − 188 = 1849

A Great Pick Me Up page 66

1. IX − VI = III; **2.** V = IV + I; **3.** I + I = III − I; **4.** X = I + IX

Finger Picking Fun page 67

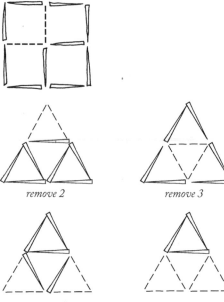

remove 2   *remove 3*

remove 4   *remove 6*

Pick of the Pack page 68

Top Secret! page 69

ENVELOPE; WHOA

It's All Greek! page 71

BECAUSE IT COMES AFTER EIGHT

THE NUMBER ONE BECAUSE IT ALWAYS WINS

Hidden Numbers page 72

1. nine; 2. three; 3. four; 4. seven; 5. one; 6. five;
7. eight; 8. ten; 9. eleven; 10. twenty

Need Some Advice? page 74

1. A stitch in time saves nine; 2. Two heads are better than one;
3. Don't count your chickens before they hatch;
4. A bird in the hand is worth two in the bush;
5. A penny saved is a penny earned.

Square Deal page 75

You are a great kid.

Test of Champions (duh!) pages 78–79

Bonus question answer: Because then it would be a foot!

Numbers with an "Attitude" page 80

A. –2; B. 2; C. –5; D. –6

Not So Square page 83

Shades of Fun:

Right on the Dot:

What Do You See? page 86

1. a beach ball hiding behind a tree; 2. a spider on a mirror;
3. a white bear in a snowstorm; 4. a look inside a shark's
mouth; 5. four elephants doing a square dance; 6. caterpillar
climbing a tree; 7. an upside-down flat tire; 8. a hot dog in
a hamburger roll

Camp Knotty Pine pages 88–89

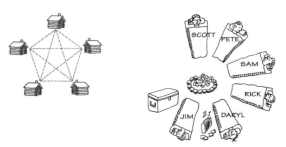

Time Teasers page 106

1. Killing time; 2. Time flies; 3. Time marches on;
4. Time on my hands

It's Only Money page 108

A. 2 dimes, 2 nickels, 4 pennies
B. 1 quarter, 3 nickels, 4 pennies OR 4 dimes, 4 pennies
C. 1 quarter, 3 dimes, 1 nickel, 3 pennies
D. 2 quarters, 2 dimes, 1 nickel, 3 pennies

Coin Trick page 111

Take the coin from the top of the vertical column and put it
on top of the coin at the bottom of that column. Then each
row will have 4 coins.

Dollars and Sense page 112

1. Move the bottom-left penny up 2 rows.
2. Move the bottom-right penny up 2 rows.
3. Move the top penny down 4 rows to the middle.

Easy Money page 113

1 quarter, 4 dimes, and 4 pennies OR;
2 quarters, 3 nickels, and 4 pennies

Making Change page 116

Move 5¢ left, 10¢ down, 1¢ right, 5¢ up, 1¢ right, 1¢ down,
5¢ left, 1¢ left, 10¢ up, 1¢ right, 1¢ down, 5¢ right, 1¢ up,
1¢ left, 1¢ left, 10¢ down, 5¢ right.

Arithmetricks page 118

A. 5637 (legs); B. 77345 (shell); C. 7738 (bell);
D. 5537 (less)

C-o-o-l Calculations page 119

One for All . . . This series emerges: 121, 12321, 123454321, 12345654321, and so on.

Going, Going Gone . . . The series of 1s reduces one by one.

Cross Number Puzzle page 132

1	2		6		2	5
5		2	3	3		0
	8	4		6	0	
1	6		2		4	4
7		6	1	1		9
3	2	2		1	4	4
	8	3		1	3	

Laugh Track page 134

A. Furry tales; **B.** It was the teacher's pet;
C. A pet peeve; **D.** It may lick you;
E. A cock-a-poodle-doo

It's a Wrap! pages 138–139

Jenn is getting the teddy bear wrapped in polka dot paper.
Jason is getting the wristwatch wrapped in striped paper.
Jud is getting the CD wrapped in smiley face paper.

Fractured Speech page 142

1. I understand how hard this task is; **2.** But before you undertook the challenge, I knew you'd do well;
3. I will be overjoyed when you get the answers right;
4. I have overheard that this is no easy feat.

Fun with Fractions: a day; $\frac{14}{14}$; $\frac{1}{4}$

Party page 144

	1	2	3	4	5
Bethany	✓				
Keesha			✓		
Ivan			✓		
Paul					✓
Samantha		✓			